PORTFOLIO/PENGUIN

DEALS ON THE GREEN

David Rynecki is the founder of Blue Heron Research Partners, a firm that conducts due diligence for investors. He previously spent fifteen years in journalism, writing about golf, investing, and Wall Street. He has written for *Time*, *Travel + Leisure Golf*, and *Golf Digest*. He spent six years as a senior writer at *Fortune*, where he discovered that most of the people he was researching were also avid golfers.

DEALS

ON THE

GREEN

LESSONS ON BUSINESS AND GOLF

FROM AMERICA'S TOP EXECUTIVES

DAVID RYNECKI

PORTFOLIO/PENGUIN

PORTFOLIO / PENGUIN

Published by the Penguin Group
Penguin Group (USA) Inc., 375 Hudson Street, New York, New York 10014, U.S.A.
Penguin Group (Canada), 90 Eglinton Avenue East, Suite 700, Toronto,
Ontario, Canada M4P 2Y3 (a division of Pearson Penguin Canada Inc.)
Penguin Books Ltd, 80 Strand, London WC2R 0RL, England
Penguin Ireland, 25 St Stephen's Green, Dublin 2, Ireland (a division of Penguin Books Ltd)
Penguin Books (Australia), 250 Camberwell Road, Camberwell, Victoria 3124, Australia
(a division of Pearson Australia Group Pty Ltd)
Penguin Group India Pvt Ltd, 11 Community Centre, Panchsheel Park,
New Delhi – 110 017, India
Penguin Group (NZ), 67 Apollo Drive, Rosedale, North Shore 0632, New Zealand
(a division of Pearson New Zealand Ltd.)
Penguin Books (South Africa) (Pty) Ltd, 24 Sturdee Avenue, Rosebank, Johannesburg 2196,
South Africa

Penguin Books Ltd, Registered Offices:
80 Strand, London WC2R 0RL, England

First published in the United States of America by Portfolio,
a member of Penguin Group (USA) Inc. 2007
This paperback edition with a new preface and two new selections ("Merrill's Man" and
"Checklist on the Dos and Don'ts of Business Golf") published 2011

1 3 5 7 9 10 8 6 4 2

THE LIBRARY OF CONGRESS HAS CATALOGED THE HARDCOVER EDITION AS FOLLOWS:

Rynecki, David.
  Deals on the green : lessons on business and golf from America's top executives / David Rynecki.
    p. cm.
  Includes index.
  ISBN 978-1-59184-155-5 (hc.)
  ISBN 978-159184-407-5 (pbk.)
  1. Success in business—United States. 2. Business networks—United States. 3. Strategic
planning—United States. 4. Business entertaining—United States. 5. Golf—Psychological
aspects. I. Title.
  HF5386.R96 2007
  658.4'09—dc22

                                                                    2006101503

Printed in the United States of America
Set in Galliard with Berthold Akzidenz Grotesk and Blair
Designed by Sabrina Bowers

To Marcia, my best friend and inspiration,

and our sons, Christopher and Carter.

And to all the office-bound hackers who dream of

being just a bit more . . .

Foreword

Analyzing why we love to play golf is like exploring the intricacies of string theory—there are so many permutations lacking scientific observation that physicists can pretty darn well say anything they like and the explanation might stick. When it comes to whacking that little white ball, the possibilities are nearly as endless. People play to relax, to be with friends, to get close to Mother Nature, to enhance business connections, to compete and excel. Gosh I don't know, the zen explanation for why we love golf could even resemble the old saw about climbing a mountain: People golf because it's there. Whatever the reason, it is the most frustrating, damnable game ever conceived—alternately elevating and depressing you within the span of mere minutes. I love golf. No, I hate it.

Personally, the reason that golf draws me to its intricate web of psychological entrapment is epitomized by a simple six-inch trophy: a chartreuse ball resting on top of its ebony base, preening on a bookshelf in the family room at our desert home. Its inscription reads, "Hole in one, March 15th, 1990, 14th hole desert course, 155 yards." Well and good, I suppose—the ace of my life—except it wasn't. It was the ace of my wife. Above the inscription rests the name Sue—not Bill Gross. It was a great shot but it wasn't *my* shot, and I guess therein lies the explanation for why I continue to tee it up. Not for a hole in one to match my wife but for the exhilaration that would accompany it. Not for another trophy on my library bookcase but for another moment of admittedly temporary triumph in the unconquerable game we know as human existence.

Golf's comparison to life itself is why so many string theory–like explanations seem to resonate on the course, in the bar on the nineteenth hole, and in David Rynecki's great book that follows. They all stick because they mimic life as we have lived and (more important) *hope* to live it. Because golf, like life itself, feeds on, no, requires hope. We approach the first tee not with a Tiger Woods–like confidence as to what will happen, but with a childlike fantasy as to what *might* happen: the 250-yard drive in the middle of the fairway, the 6 iron to within 10 feet, the downhill putt curling in on the low side of the cup, the circle on the scorecard signifying a birdie three. A hole in one would be great; but absent the miraculous, I hope for that perfect birdie and then that close-to-perfect round. Any or all of these possibilities lead to temporary triumph, momentary exhilaration, and the sense of mastering your own fate instead of vice versa.

In golf, as in life, however, success as we individually define it usually results from a combination of inspirational hope and perspirational practice. For me, it wouldn't be enough to get that hole in one or birdie without working for it. Golf, like life, is best played with preparation and lots of time at the range. As a matter of fact, I may have put in more hours on the range than the course. While that may not sound like much fun, I can assure you that the banana slice that characterized my game in its infancy was even less so. Learning to swing correctly took more time than the piano lessons my mother forced on me until I was 15. Practice boy, practice. As it turned out, piano practice wasn't my ticket to Carnegie Hall, but the range was my pass to the AT&T Pro Am in 2001. For an amateur golfer, that's about as good as it gets. And who needs a hole in one when you've walked up the eighteenth hole at Pebble with Tiger Woods in your foursome on Sunday afternoon? Well, I do, and I guess that's my point. Tiger was wonderful, but that moment is part of my past. Trophies, even mental ones, can't compare to the exhilaration of the moment, the thrill of victory, and yes, the agony of missing a three-footer. Nor can they compete with the hope for an ace or even a second Sunday with Tiger, the next time with a few more pars and perhaps a birdie on the eighteenth. The crowd wouldn't really give much of a damn, but you fantasize that the whole world's watching.

As David Rynecki points out, golf is a wonderful game that teaches you about yourself and those around you. Character, resolve, and response under pressure, all lie exposed for any and all to observe on the greens and fairways of courses everywhere. But however we individually meet these tests, hope remains the common denominator. And don't just take my word for it. Remember that chartreuse ball sitting atop my wife's hole-in-one trophy? Ugly is the only word to describe it, but it was the ball that went in on that fateful March day and so there it rests. Still even my wife, Sue, who cares much less about golf than I do, treats it as a symbolic arrow toward her future on the links, and not her past. I know because every time we play a par 3 now, she reaches into her bag for a spankin'-new white Titleist, tees it up just so, and swings for another magical hole in one that will surely top the first—if only because of the color of the ball. Golf is just that way.

BILL GROSS,
chief investment officer, Pimco

Preface

Friends often ask me if I've ever done my own deal on the green. What I tell them is that I have never teed it up expecting some business magic to happen. Yet that has been the result more times than I can remember. The relationships I've formed as a result of golf include some of my closest friends in business.

Case in point: After *Deals on the Green* was first published in 2007, I was hanging out in the locker room at my golf club in South Carolina when I met this friendly fellow named Mitch Weiner. Mitch happens to run a successful dental practice in Maryland. We soon became golf buddies. Though never my intention, Mitch has become a fantastic source of information about what it takes to run a business. I frequently call him for advice. He even introduced me to a new client and a new business partner during matches. And each time Mitch and I tee it up, we spend large portions of the round comparing notes about the issues we face as entrepreneurs. It didn't start out that way but it certainly has helped me become a smarter businessperson.

Now that's not to say the golf course is the only place to get to know people. Indeed, after several prominent CEO-golfers lost their jobs during the 2008 financial crisis when they were allegedly putting while the economy imploded, it might seem politically incorrect to be seen on a fairway.

Yet there is no denying that golf remains one of the best ways to truly learn about people. In the pages that follow, you'll see examples of this very thing. I've been fortunate to know some people who carry a lot of weight in business. Some of them are as fantastic on the golf course as they are dynamic in the boardroom. What golf has offered me is a window into their personalities. It is true that 18 holes can teach you more about whether you like someone than you can ever glean by sitting across the table from that person. This isn't about whether your playing partner goes for it on a par five or leaves birdie putts short. It has everything to do with whether you enjoy spending time together.

Contents

DEALS

ON THE

GREEN

Introduction

MY INTRODUCTION TO THE THRILLING, challenging, frustrating, cruel, and beautiful game of golf came when the business end of a 7 iron collided with my left cheek. I was five years old, in my first year of summer camp in Maine, and wouldn't have made it to six if the rusty old club swung by a fellow camper had impacted just a little higher. I can remember watching the boy's backswing and follow-through and wondering why he wasn't stopping. Years later, I'm sure my parents still feel guilty whenever I tell the story.

That painful, blood-filled thwack began a lifelong love affair. This might sound a bit counterintuitive, but I just *had* to play—if only to get back at that 7 iron. By age 12, I had nagged my father so much that he finally started taking me to a nine-holer in Walpole, New Hampshire. I remember my first swing. The banana ball flew 75 yards and never made it more than four feet off the ground. My fingers stung from the mishit. But I was hooked—er, sliced. Throughout my teenage years, I'd spend weekends at the local mountain course that we joined in Springfield, Vermont, playing 27 to 36 holes a day. I wasn't very good. But as any golfer appreciates, you don't need to be good to fantasize about nipping Jack Nicklaus with a birdie on 18. Later, I earned a spot as the seventh man of my college's weak Division One team. I remember walking into the clubhouse after a match in which I shot 106 on a 7600-yard course. My teammates, none of whom broke 85, gasped when they heard my score. "But it was a great 106," I said.

I suppose it never occurred to me that golf would be a part of my professional life. The closest indication came from one of those tests you take during your senior year of high school—the ones intended to tell you what you should do for a career. My test told me that I should either sell golf balls or join the navy. I chose neither and instead became a journalist. Golf remained distinct from my work—it was the thing I did when I could sneak away from under the boss's nose.

It was really happenstance that taught me how valuable golf would be to my career and it began with three words: I know Nordy. Now, I don't actually know Nordy's last name or even if I've spelled his first name right or much else about him. But this book probably wouldn't even exist were it not for the fact that I met Nordy. So who is Nordy? Some years ago, I was fortunate to be an unaccompanied guest of a family friend who belonged to the Cypress Point Golf Club on the Monterey Peninsula. In addition to being the most beautiful stretch of fairways, greens, and crashing surf in the world, Cypress is also an ultraexclusive club. The 300 or so members include the biggest names in business. Because most of these members live far from the club and visit only once or twice a year, the rules allow members to arrange for unaccompanied guests. This is as much to maintain a professional corps of caddies as it is to help pay some of the bills. Cypress caddies are the smartest, most knowledgeable caddies this side of Scotland. They live and breathe the course. And I was lucky to have met one of the best of the bunch. Nordy was my caddie. And he was a great caddie. We sank more long putts that day than any round I've played before or since. I even holed a bunker shot.

A few months after that round, I was sitting in a conference room inside the Time-Life Building in New York listening to brokerage founder Charles Schwab explain why investors needed his company. I was a writer at *Fortune* at the time and my job was to cover financial markets. That meant getting to know Wall Street CEOs who didn't exactly want to spill their guts to a reporter. Most couldn't relate to journalists, nor could most journalists relate to them. And so it was a really dull conversation. All the editors and writers in the room looked to be falling asleep as Schwab droned on about various plans for the business. I wondered what happened to the dynamic, visionary CEO I had heard about—the one who transformed investing by making it easier for average Americans to own stocks. Afterward, it was my job to escort Schwab to the elevator. As we were walking, I casually mentioned having played Cypress Point to see what he would say. I knew Schwab was a long-time member. "I'd have never made it around without the caddy, a guy named Nordy," I told him.

Schwab stopped in his tracks. "I know Nordy," he said. He began telling me all about his most recent round at the club. He was more animated than I'd ever seen him. I started mixing in a few questions about business, which he answered with equal excitement. At the end of this conversation, he shook my hand and said, "So you understand me." I could practically hear the gates unlocking.

I was about to discover what generations of business people

have known: that no matter how sophisticated the tools become—the e-mails and teleconferencing, the BlackBerrys and PowerPoint presentations—golf remains the true communications hub of American business. It is the great and peaceful forum where movers and shakers can meet, spend time together, and decide whether they want to do business in the future. It is the place where there is no need for a Myers-Briggs test, because the game brings out a person's true character.

This book is designed to take you inside the secret world of golf and business—to remove some of the myths but also to pay homage to the sport and its most passionate players. It is not a how to win business instructional but it does contain certain lessons about what is required to succeed in both golf and business—namely, friendship, imagination, tenacity, multitasking, guts, passion, and compassion—along with stories about people who embody these ideals. You'll read about successful people whose devotion and respect for the game have led to their success in business.

Now, up-close glimpses of this world are rare. It is, not surprisingly, a world that does not welcome outsiders. And yet despite lacking financial resources and social pedigree, I was able to get inside the gates of dozens of the greatest clubs in the country and see what really goes on when the titans of industry and finance get together. I did this without compromising my ethics or pretending that I was someone I am not or promising to write puff pieces. It was all so simple once I understood that golf could be my tool. I realized that these people who seemed so difficult to reach were really quite accessible if I chose the right words and let them know that I spoke the same language. The language of golf became my greatest reporting tool, and over the years has enabled me to probe into the business operations of some of the world's most secretive corporate chieftains. Mind you, this was not about sucking up. My goal was always to write a truthful article. But because we were always able to find common ground on the golf course we could also speak with greater candor.

Soon after the experience with Schwab I was at Pebble Beach playing with the CEO of the Knight-Ridder newspaper chain, Tony Ridder. We were having a blast—I was with my dad and Ridder was with his wife. I mentioned that I'd just spent time with Schwab and Ridder told me the two were good friends. After those few words we were comfortable swapping stories. He showed me Schwab's house adjacent to the green of a par-3 and told me how he and Schwab were going to be teamed in a member-guest event at a Montana golf community Schwab had financed. Mrs. Ridder told me all about the kitchen Mrs. Schwab had built. Ridder went on to offer his opinion about whether Schwab could rebuild his company after the implosion of the stock market. Along the way, we ran into the infamous investment banker Frank Quattrone, who had just been indicted for breaking securities laws. A blustery man with a thick mustache and potbelly, Quattrone lived in a mansion on one of the holes and was playing in the foursome just ahead of us. When he saw Ridder, he walked up and immediately lashed into the newspaper owner for the critical articles Knight-Ridder's *San Jose Mercury News* had written about him. Ridder defended his reporter and Quattrone stormed off. I got to see it all and later used the scene in an article.

This was more than a colorful scene. It was an example of how the golf course can teach us about other people and ourselves. These are the displays of character both good and bad—the tendency of one player to cheat and another to call a penalty on himself, the anger of one player after a wayward shot and the earnest glee for a playing partner's 30-footer for birdie. Such actions also include the way we are observed treating others. Do we speak kindly to the caddies or dismiss them as servants? Do we act rudely to players in front who are moving too slowly? Does our playing partner spend the entire round pitching business when we just want to have fun? Ultimately, the beauty of golf as a tool in business is that it requires time—an entire morning or afternoon—and that it is one of the only activities in which we have the chance to spend time actually learning about another person with the only distraction being the sound of birds. In so doing, we learn not just lessons in business but lessons in life.

LESSON

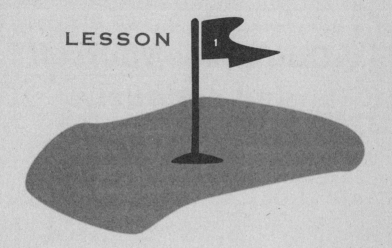

Don't take yourself too seriously.

Bill and Warren's
Excellent Adventure

ON A BRILLIANT GEORGIA AFTERNOON, two men were walking up a steep hill toward the final green of the Augusta National Golf Club. One was lanky with a mop of brown hair, the other stocky with graying hair and a slight limp to his gait. They both dressed in inexpensive-looking plaid pants and wore glasses too large for their faces. After sinking their final putts, the two shook hands with their caddies and went inside the clubhouse for a game of bridge.

"Who are those two geeks?" a guest remembered asking his host.

"Oh, that's only Warren Buffett and Bill Gates," the host replied with a hint of sarcasm because the guest didn't recognize the world's two richest men.

Neither Buffett, chairman of Berkshire Hathaway and the

greatest investor of the last 100 years, nor Gates, founder of Microsoft, would seem like the poster boys for corporate golf. Both have 20-plus handicaps. Buffett, now around 76, started golfing as a kid, sometimes sneaking onto the Elmwood Park golf course near where he grew up in Omaha, Nebraska. He was a caddy and played on his high school's golf team. He likes to joke that his game peaked when he was 13. Between 1985 and 2006, he posted only 20 scores at his home course, the Omaha Country Club—breaking 90 just once and shooting as high as 115. He barely touches a club anymore and prefers to visit with friends and play bridge. Gates, who is barely 50, picked up the game in his mid-thirties and has worked diligently to lower his handicap to around 20. Like Buffett, his passion is also bridge.

Yet despite their unimpressive golf skills, Buffett and Gates embody everything that we should admire about the game. One of the main reasons is that they're fun. Several top *Fortune* 500 CEOs I've interviewed have told me that Gates and Buffett (along with Arnold Palmer) would be in their dream foursome because they'd have so many laughs. Charles Schwab told me that once he was teamed with Buffett in a friendly match against Bill Gates and investment banker George Roberts. After Schwab's side lost the match, he asked Buffett for the money. Buffett, who is worth in excess of $40 billion, didn't have the $4 in his wallet to pay off the bet. (Buffett once told me he didn't recall not having the cash. "A lot of people have those stories about me," he said.) Another top business leader, Tom Mendoza of technology company Network Appliance, paid $650,000 in 2000 to play golf with Tiger Woods—largely because during the bidding Buffett stood up and offered to caddy for the winner. Mendoza later said his round with Tiger was a blast because Buffett was so much fun. Jack Welch, arguably the greatest corporate golfer of all time, told *Golf Digest* about a match in Nantucket with Buffett, Gates, and a close friend who had sold his company to Buffett's Berkshire Hathaway. Buffett parred the first hole and Gates declared him the winner of the entire match. It seemed that the two men had a standing competition that whoever made the first par, won. Welch was miffed but the story underscores the value of camaraderie over competition outside the office.

Now a lot of people want to talk trash about these two. One story has it that Gates and Buffett were scolded for playing bridge instead of interacting with members at an invitational event at the Cypress Point Golf Club. Another story states that Gates was kept out of Augusta National for several years because he said publicly that he wanted to be a member. Buffett was already a member and undoubtedly had some influence over the club's decision to finally make Gates a member. The truth is that most of that talk is just jealousy.

The reason I think Buffett and Gates embody what is great about golf—and the reason so many people want to play with them—is that they don't take themselves seriously when they are on the course. They're the best in their respective professions and yet don't try to take that to golf. They're happy having a good time. How many playing partners have you met who aren't that way? I don't have enough fingers and toes to count the stories I have about *Fortune* 500 CEOs, iconic investment bankers, and aspiring corporate chieftains who have behaved badly. How many people have you met who demand to be treated like royalty? Pretension is a dead giveaway for insecurity, and what makes Gates and Buffett so special is that they are uniquely secure individuals. They simply don't care if they look foolish hitting a little white ball along tightly mowed grass. That is a lesson for us all.

LESSON 2

Don't listen to the gallery.

Merrill's Man

T WAS A HOT, HUMID JUNE DAY at the Golf Club of Purchase, located a short ride from Manhattan. I stood on the velvety practice range hitting balls waiting for my host to arrive for what I knew would be a fun round. A caddy hovered in the background ready to wipe every blade of grass off my club until it sparkled.

Just before noon, my host arrived with a box of logo balls in one hand and the other extended for a hearty handshake. Stan O'Neal wasn't coming from the office. It had been more than two years since he had been fired from his job as CEO of Merrill Lynch. During those two years, the global economy had teetered on the edge of collapse, unemployment in the United States had surged and the stock market had sunk more dramatically than any of us imagined possible. And one of the people blamed for all this—the Wall Street CEO often cited as the last to know and the

first to go—was now pulling a wedge from his bag and preparing
to take a few practice swings.

The world had certainly changed since the first time Stan and
I teed it up. That was in early 2004, at the height of his career at
Merrill. He had come a long way from tiny Wedowee, Alabama.
The grandson of a man who was born into slavery, Stan's family
had a small farm and from an early age Stan had helped work the
fields. He attended a one-room schoolhouse built by his grandfather. It was during the worst part of segregation in Alabama. His
father eventually got a job at a General Motors plant in Georgia
and moved the family to a housing project in Atlanta. Stan showed
promise as a student and earned entrance to the General Motors
Institute (now Kettering University). As part of the program, he
alternated between school and working at his father's plant. After
college, he went to work as a supervisor at the plant. He excelled
and GM paid his way through Harvard Business School. He
stayed with GM for eight years, moving upward into finance
roles, until leaving for Merrill Lynch in 1986 where he began a
steady upward march.

Stan quickly rose through the ranks at Merrill. As CFO, he
led efforts to stabilize the firm as well as the rest of Wall Street
during the 1998 Russian financial crisis. He then took over Merrill's massive army of stockbrokers—a controversial move because he had never been a broker—and restored the business to
profitability. After weathering a nasty succession battle, he was
made president shortly before the 9/11 attacks. With Merrill's
headquarters just feet from the World Trade Center, Stan and
then-CEO David Komansky stayed behind to make sure employees got out safely. Not all did. Stan eventually fled on foot with a
group of coworkers. When one of his managers fell and injured
himself, Stan carried the man's son (who had come to visit that
day) several blocks north. It was harrowing; for days afterward,

Stan was haunted by the memory of looking back at the fallen towers and seeing people around him simply sit down and cry. Yet within hours, he had gathered top lieutenants to begin planning for the aftermath. Merrill would be without headquarters for months.

This is when I first met Stan. I remember having heard that he was quite cold and aloof. This was how rivals at Merrill portrayed him and how reporters liked to write about him. He was a robot in a suit, a bean counter who liked to fire people. Some rivals at Merrill called Stan "Mullah Omar" and dubbed his band of allies the "Taliban." During the CEO succession battle, rivals staged a campaign much like a political race in which they planted stories in the media about how Stan was out golfing with key board members and insisting that he could never lead.

Like a lot of other journalists, I loved the image of the cold, calculating executive running a firm long known for its beloved backslapping Irish CEOs. Indeed, of all the companies I covered as a journalist, Merrill was the most fun because it was such a mess. You name the crisis—Russian financial, Orange County's bankruptcy—Merrill had a hand in it. The firm that took Wall Street to Main Street was also run more like a sprawling empire than a lean fighting machine. Even on the inside, it was disorganized. It was like a soap opera with senior executives constantly stabbing each other in the back through leaks to the media. Stan came in and fixed a lot of those problems. But he played office politics and the media game poorly. In interviews with journalists, he came across as wooden, using terms like "corporate DNA" that seemed straight out of a management textbook. Internally, he fired some incompetent but well-liked managers while failing to see that their departures would make him seem mean even though those executives should have been dismissed years earlier.

Even after seeing him deal so impressively with the aftermath of 9/11 (I spent part of the following week with him as he worked multiple phones and never lost his cool), I remained among those who praised his successes but criticized his leadership skills. I even wrote an article that compared his replacing rival executives after he became CEO to the Kremlin's erasing the photos of Politburo members.

So what changed my mind? To an extent, it was that I got tired of the backstabbing. On one occasion, a former senior executive at Merrill called me with a "tip" that Stan had just ordered the company to spend $3 million refurbishing the company jet simply because he didn't like the bathroom. I did some investigating and found out that contrary to the image of decadence this executive tried to convey, the true story was that Stan and a top lieutenant had been on their way to Japan when the jet's toilet broke down for the umpteenth time. Stan and others had to pee in a makeshift bowl until they landed in Tokyo. As a result, the company that serviced the plane had to make repairs—for far less than $3 million.

There were other revelations too, little signs that Stan actually had a sense of humor. I also began to see evidence that he was far from aloof; he was a mentor to many inside the company. But what really changed my mind was playing golf with him.

I've learned a lot playing golf with Stan. Unlike a lot of CEOs, Stan didn't have his secretary dial the phone and then keep me waiting the first time we arranged to play. I almost thought he was joking when he called me up asking if I wanted to meet at his club.

"You have to promise me one thing," he said.

"Okay."

"That you never write about me again."

It occurred to me that he might be trying to spin me. CEOs

are always trying to get on the nice side of journalists and it made sense to me that he would do the same. But he never tried to spin me. We started on the first tee, the only group on the course. For the first few holes, we did the usual small talk. I asked a few questions. He offered some basic answers. He seemed uncomfortable, which was strange to me because he was one of the most powerful men in business and I was just a reporter. We seemed to spend most of the time sizing each other up. By the sixth hole, we decided to put a little money on the game—$2 a hole. Since we played about the same, no one got strokes. I felt pretty confident just because Stan kept missing short putts—and my flat stick was on fire. Soon, with the competition heating up, Stan asked me a question:

"You wrote that I use jargon when I speak," he said referencing an article I had written for *Fortune*. "I didn't know what that meant."

I was a little surprised because he wasn't challenging the description. He was trying to learn. So I explained to him that he seemed frozen in public and often fell back on phrases cooked up by his PR staff. He stopped momentarily and then added, "I really want to understand."

"But you don't care what people think, do you?"

"That's not what I meant. I don't care about noise. But I care about being better at my job. I care about not confusing people."

So I explained what I meant and we seemed to develop a bond. I could see him changing from uptight to calm. His real self was coming out. Suddenly, he was comfortable talking about himself. I asked him how he started playing. "I frankly don't even know when I became aware of what golf was. When I was growing up in Alabama, I can't ever remember thinking about or even seeing golf in any way, shape, or form. We didn't have a television so we couldn't even see it that way, and we didn't have many newspapers around us."

But by 1997, as his corporate ascension was fully under way, he decided to give the game a try. Some friends were developing a course and needed members. "I wondered why I would ever want to join a golf course. I thought it was a silly sport. I had the disdain many tennis players have for golf. Eventually I had kids who were five or six, and I thought they might get interested, and I thought it might be good for my career at some point, and I thought I might get too old to play tennis. So I joined the club and then bought a set of clubs, and from 1997 to 2000 I played 10 rounds."

Then candidly he added, "It wasn't love at first sight."

What won him over was that the game was so frustrating—the fact that it couldn't be mastered easily and that hard work could make him improve. "I started to apply myself and take lessons and golf somehow became more than just an artifice or mechanism to integrate myself into my business. It became a passion. Golf seemed like a metaphor for my life. I could be competitive by challenging myself and also spend time away from conference tables learning about other people. I believe in enriching my life—I'm not talking about financially, but intellectually and socially and artistically. The richness of life is from possibilities and that is golf."

I ended up losing to Stan that day after he pressed me on 17 and 18 and ended up taking $15 from me.

Between that first round and the next, a lot changed. Stan went from being a hero to being persona non grata on Wall Street. In the fall of 2008, Merrill disclosed its huge exposure to the U.S. housing market. That led to massive losses. The firm's market value evaporated. Merrill was acquired by Bank of America for $50 billion in 2009. A year earlier, even before much of this became public, the board fired Stan for trying to sell Merrill to Bank of America, whose CEO happened to be a fellow member of Augusta National. The price Lewis and O'Neal discussed was $100 billion. Though Stan walked away with a $160 million package, his reputation was decimated.

Books and articles about what happened have portrayed Stan as the isolated CEO who golfed while his lieutenants destroyed the firm. I'm sure some elements of what has been written are true. I always thought of Stan as someone who is much better during a crisis than a boom. After fixing many of Merrill's problems in the first part of the decade, he probably should have moved onto a new opportunity. There was talk that he was in line to be Treasury Secretary. Instead, he rode the full cycle.

In hindsight, it might even make sense to pretend that I feel differently—that I think he was a terrible CEO. That is certainly what many commentators and former colleagues have done. But I've also seen a side of Stan that might surprise most people. Of all the *Fortune* 500 CEOs I've met, he's the only one who ever actually listened or asked a question. On the golf course, I've found our experiences fun and enlightening. Our conversations range from the economy to his business ventures to charity. It was this way even before he left Merrill. Most people expect Stan to be aloof. I've found him engaging. Even while he was still CEO, we spent an afternoon on the golf course talking about my plans for starting a business. He encouraged me and gave me advice.

The last time we played, on that humid day at Purchase, I asked him about what went wrong at Merrill. He seemed to say that it was all one huge mess. He blamed himself for not recognizing the complete risks sooner. But I also asked him why he wasn't doing more to explain what happened and why he was letting people who were far more responsible get away with blaming him and accepting none of the responsibility for themselves. Old golf companions like Jim Gorman, now the CEO of Morgan Stanley, had been architects of Merrill's strategy and now said everything that went wrong was Stan's fault.

He thought about my question momentarily. "I can't change what happened," he said. "Who would listen anyway?"

And then he turned to his ball and smacked it 260 yards down the middle.

Golf is about
playing by the rules

Curt Culver is possly the best CEO golfer in the *Fortune* 500. Culver, who is CEO of mortgage insurer MGIC, has made a career out of combining golf and business. He's also the part owner with his family of Culver's Butterburgers & Custard, a popular midwestern restaurant chain with 300 locations in 16 states. Curt told me why he likes to take prospective new hires out golfing before making a final decision.

"Golf teaches you about a person's reaction to adversity—how they deal competitively with situations—because with golf there is such an easy mechanism to take advantage of the rules. I'm not worried about their skill as a player, but rather how they conduct themselves, as golf, like business and life, will test you in a multitude of ways. Some react by throwing clubs or cursing wildly, while others react more honorably. Obviously those who react with dignity are the individuals I would choose to do business with or to hire. Golf is a game of principles, and they are the same principles that are practiced in life and business. If a person abuses the rules of golf, I guarantee they will also abuse them in life and business."

LESSON 3

Look for opportunities that others can't see.

Fireman's Folly

PAUL **FIREMAN SAYS** he does not believe in vengeance. And when he tells the story about how two decades ago his membership application was rejected from the uppercrust Oyster Harbors golf club in Cape Cod, he insists the event didn't affect him in the least.

It was the late 1980s and Fireman was already famous for having turned Reebok into a global brand. Fireman and his wife had bought a house just a par 3 from the stately gates of Oyster Harbors, a course that was designed by the famed Donald Ross and was reputed to be among the most exclusive in New England. Some friends who already belonged to the club suggested he apply. So he filled out the paperwork and turned it into the membership committee expecting to meet for interviews. Time passed and there were no calls to schedule a meeting. After months of waiting, word trickled back—nothing official, mind you—that

Fireman was being blackballed. Perhaps it was because he ran such a well-known company and the club preferred to keep a low profile. Or maybe it was his reputation as a blunt-spoken (read: loud-mouthed) CEO. Or that he represented so-called new money. There were even suggestions that Fireman wasn't wanted because he was Jewish and the club had no Jewish members at the time. (The club refuses to discuss any of this.) As for Fireman, a man who doesn't normally guard his opinions, he is reticent to explain what went wrong. "There are no hard feelings," he said.

In fact, Fireman insists the slight had no impact on him. He continues to live next door to Oyster Harbors and maintains cordial relations with some of its members. What he did next is nonetheless instructive. After learning he was being blackballed, he withdrew his membership application. He then paid $9 million out of his own pocket to buy a nearby semi-private golf club that had fallen into bankruptcy. He poured millions of dollars into redesigning the holes, landscaping flats into hilly terrain, and covering the grounds with flowers. He refurbished the shingle-style clubhouse and built guest cottages, added a spa and amenities. And then he rechristened Willowbend Golf Club as a private venue. Fireman went one step further: He made sure there was no membership committee save for the benevolent dictator who owned the course. Fireman personally assembled a membership that included Jews, blacks, Asians, and women. He invited golfers who belonged to the club when it was a virtual dog track to stay on even though many were not in the same tax bracket as the newer recruits. Fireman made sure that every membership decision was done in the open and insisted that anyone who tried to blackball another member be expelled. "I hate blackballing," he said. "It is an ignorant practice from an old era."

Next Fireman took the team of architects, landscapers, and marketers he had assembled to rebuild Willowbend and formed a golf course development company that to date has built resort clubs and residential communities in Arizona and Puerto Rico— each with the a similar down-home, no cliques style—and amassed holdings estimated at $2 billion.

But all this was just a prelude. In 2006, at 61, and just a year after his career at Reebok had ended (he sold out to Adidas in 2005 for $3.8 billion), Fireman unveiled his most ambitious project to date. In 2000 Fireman had purchased a strip of oozing, chemical-filled sludge on the New Jersey shoreline opposite Manhattan and the Statue of Liberty. The site, laced with PCBs and other toxic waste, was owned by several oil companies. After a $150 million investment, the land has been scrubbed clean. Barren flats have been turned into 55-foot bluffs. The rolling fairways are lined with full-grown maples, honey locusts, flowering pear trees, and willows. At an initiation fee of $500,000, members are being recruited from the ranks of finance, politics, entertainment, and sports. And the newly named Liberty National Golf Club is already being talked about as the site of a major golf championship.

But this is more than a story about yet another mogul like Donald Trump or Steve Wynn who decided that the quickest path to self-deification is to build a golf course. Fireman's Liberty National is less a personal tribute than a tribute to the self-made person, the man or woman who defies the status quo. As Bob Kraft, owner of the New England Patriots and a friend of Fireman's put it, "Paul is the quintessential hometown boy who made good."

As anyone who has worked for him at Reebok can attest, Fireman can be charming and humorous at one moment, steely and gruff at the next. He seems less like a major CEO than a small-business owner. Deep down, he remains an entrepreneur who is unafraid of risks and can confound those around him.

Even as a young man, he chose less ordinary routes. After his father joined a local country club named Thorny Lea, Fireman became a caddy so he could earn his own money. Later, while helping run the family sporting goods business, Fireman could sometimes seem too demanding and at other times too dreamy. Part of that reflected a frustration that the family business had a limited future. And he was right. By the 1970s, business was stagnant. Fishing rods, after all, were only going to get him so far. He began traveling to sporting goods trade shows in search of a business opportunity.

It was at one of these shows in Chicago that Fireman discovered a little-known company that made hand-stitched sneakers for Olympic athletes. Though Reebok's sales were miniscule, Fireman invested $35,000 in acquiring the North American distribution rights. Even that amount was a major sacrifice. The family had to take out a mortgage on their house to finance growing the business and his wife, Phyllis, had to take on a job selling encyclopedias. The bet paid off, however, and by the mid-1980s Fireman had turned Reebok into a global brand by introducing a new soft-leather aerobics sneaker. By 1984, Fireman had purchased the entire company and taken Reebok public, all the while frenetically playing the roles of sneaker designer, marketer, and even sports agent. He personally lobbied athletes for their endorsements and made sure that Reebok was the sneaker of choice in sports like football. He could also be a visionary when it came to the workplace. After learning about human rights abuses in Asia, for example, Fireman instituted a new plan for elevating working conditions and hired a chief human rights officer, who reported directly to the CEO.

Reebok was never a model of management success like General Electric. It was more of an R&D and marketing operation, and this was a direct result of Fireman's tendency to run hot and cold. It was natural, therefore, that Fireman's passion for the business would wane as Reebok became more established. By the late 1980s, Fireman was already testing alternative ventures including Willowbend. Throughout the 1990s he was an on-again, off-again CEO. Increasingly, he could see that Reebok was at a competitive disadvantage to the larger sporting-equipment conglomerates. And then along came Adidas with an offer to buy Reebok for $3.8 billion in 2005, valuing the Fireman family's stake at around $800 million.

It was one of those pristine Cape Cod mornings when the sky is cloudless and the fairways at Willowbend appear to be made from velvet. Fireman was standing at the tee with a driver in his hands waiting for his son, Dan, to play his shot. Dan helps run the golf operation and, like his father, is a thickly built man with a wicked sense of humor and an eye for some side competition. "Bet you $1 on the longest drive," the elder Fireman propositioned in a thick Boston accent. The son accepted the challenge and addressed the ball. Whispering to another player, Fireman made a prediction: "He's going to snap hook this. Look at where he has his hands."

Sure enough the ball soared to the left. The elder Fireman, a 7 handicapper, stabbed his tee into the ground and confidently smacked his ball 240 yards down the middle. He smiled victoriously but without too much fanfare. These sorts of bets are part of the routine with Paul Fireman. He craves action and challenges and has a hard time keeping focused without a goal to work toward. He'll propose bets just to keep from being bored, like when a few holes later he suggested that another playing partner couldn't hit an oak tree just a few yards away. He won that bet, too. He then spent the next three holes administering golf lessons to me, his hapless partner, until he finally lost another bet and had just as big a laugh as when he won.

By the middle of the round, however, Fireman appeared agitated. For several holes, he had been talking about those slivers of grass and dirt known as divots that are created when a club cuts into the ground as it impacts with a ball. Ordinarily, players replace the divots so the grass can grow back. But whoever was playing in front had not been abiding by this well-known rule. Chunks of grass littered the fairway. Fireman was incensed by this not only because the rule breakers continued to leave behind fresh evidence but the divots themselves were long and thin—a sign that the culprits were accomplished players and not weekend hackers who didn't know any better. Fireman soon flagged down one of the course pros. It's the lack of respect for the game and the course and its owner that really had him fuming. "Get all your assistant pros out here and tell them to watch people coming up the fairway," he demanded. "They're tearing the crap out of it."

Then he turned to me. "Come on," he urged. And moments later, we were both crouched beneath low-hanging branches spying on a group walking up an adjacent fairway who Fireman suspected of committing the injustice. But when each player replaced their divots, Fireman drove us away sheepishly. "When I find out who did this, they'll need to find a new club to join," he said. "I'm going to rip their fucking hearts out."

Soon after, he was back to his old tricks—this time challenging me to a bet. If I could break 40 over the final eight holes of the course off the black tees, he pledged to donate a foursome at Liberty National to my favorite charity. If he won, I needed to do the same for him with my own club at Kiawah Island. "But you won't do it," he said. "Not the way you're swinging."

The comments, to be honest, got under my skin—and he knew it. I'd been interviewing him all morning and not paying attention to my game. So I put away my pad and pen and reached for a 5 iron. We were on a par-3 with a long shot over wetlands.

Fireman missed the green with his shot. He proceeded to tell me all the places not to hit, probably thinking this was needling me to great effect. But this time something overcame me and I struck my shot better than any in my life. The ball stopped like a dart three feet from the hole. Over the final holes, I was a par machine. Fireman seemed increasingly annoyed by my success.

"You're a hustler," he told me. "I can't believe you hustled me."

"Maybe," I said.

Then he busted up laughing because he realized that, on this day, I had gotten the best of him. It was a day of vintage Fireman.

So how did all this—Reebok, Oyster Harbors, and Willowbend—lead to the most expensive golf course ever built? The story goes that in 1998 a real estate adviser named Roland Bates, whose company Fireman had purchased, drove Fireman to the strip of land along the New Jersey shore. Fireman walked around for five minutes, gazed at the Statue of Liberty and the Manhattan skyline, and then sat back in the car. "Do the deal," he said. It took three years for all the pieces to come together. Fireman retained architects Tom Kite and Bob Cupp, who had been hired by the oil company owners to design a course in the mid-1990s. But he also made sure that Kite and Cupp had a generous budget and ample access to Fireman's existing golf development team. He struck an agreement to have famed chef Tom Colicchio run the clubhouse restaurant and commissioned the building of a high-speed yacht to carry members and guests from Wall Street to the first tee. "Paul is one of those people who can seize an opportunity when all everyone else sees is risk and turn that into a vision," Bates told me.

Walking along the newly planted fairways with Fireman, I got the distinct feeling that this is more than a business deal. The course was now a lush green, and four man-made streams created additional hazards. A light breeze was blowing in from off the

Atlantic. Fireman seemed aware of every aspect of the project—that the fairways are a custom-grown dwarf bluegrass and the greens are made from a type of bent grass known as A4. He can tell you the type of stone the cart paths are cut from and is personally involved in recruiting the best caddies. He had already played the course dozens of times in his mind and knew that on the eighteenth tee, when you are directly facing the Manhattan skyline, you need to aim your shot to the right and allow the breeze to move the ball toward the center, because anything too far right is dead in New York Harbor and too far left is in the deep fescue.

In building what he envisions as an American St. Andrews—a majestic course set amid buildings—Fireman is building a tribute to the self-made man who has largely been unwanted in the most elite private clubs. His club will not be an old money spot like Deepdale, which caters to the CEO crowd, or even Augusta National, which has an assortment of CEOs but is largely comprised of the southern aristocracy. There will be no committees at Fireman's club. Fireman's membership consists of men like former New York mayor Rudy Giuliani, financier Ken Langone, and Patriots' owner Robert Kraft—men who probably never imagined growing up that they'd be in such a position. Because of that there is talk—whispers, really—that Liberty National is the "new money" Augusta. No cultured person, this chatter goes, would want to be seen teeing off by tourists cruising on the ferry or viewing from the top of the statue.

All that, of course, is probably just fine with Paul Fireman.

LESSON

4

You can play Augusta . . . with a little luck.

Five Steps to Crashing
the Gates

I'M GOING TO TELL YOU a story that will make you want to cry—and check your voice mail. One morning I arrived at my office, sat down at my computer, and noticed the little red light blinking on my telephone. It was Monday and I'd been away since Thursday and had deliberately avoided checking my messages. I punched in my password and the friendly computer voice announced I had one message received on Thursday afternoon.

"Dave, this is _____. We're headed down to Augusta for the weekend and we just lost our fourth. I thought you might want to join us. We can pick you up in the morning and fly down on my plane."

I remember the numbing sensation that filled my brain as I played back the message. It was from a source who was an Augusta member. Hoping that he meant *this coming* weekend and not last weekend, I called him at work. Sure enough, he meant the weekend that was now gone.

"Where would we have stayed?" I asked, already knowing the answer.

"In a cabin," he told me. "We had a great time. Played eighteen each day."

"Maybe we can try again sometime," I said nervously.

"Absolutely," he answered reassuringly.

That was two years ago and I've never gotten another invitation. If my source is reading this book, I hope he will call. I doubt he will. When you're an Augusta member, there's no shortage of people willing to play with you. In fact, when you're an Augusta PR person there's no shortage of requests either. I was once visiting the course for an article and got to tour the facilities and even stand beside the eighteenth green. I had my clubs in my trunk on the chance that my tour guide would invite me to tee it up. He didn't.

That is not to suggest we'll never get our chance. I'm often asked how to get onto the world's greatest private golf courses. I'd like to offer you some suggestions:

Be Charitable

One of the easiest ways to get onto an exclusive course is to find a charity that holds an event there. The Cystic Fibrosis Foundation holds an annual fund-raiser at Winged Foot, for example. Other charities hold tournaments at Oakmont, Baltusrol, and Pine Valley, to name a few.

Another route is to attend a charity auction. What happens is club members are allowed to put up rounds of golf for a good cause. So keep an eye open for fund-raisers where you will find attendees bidding for access. Local philanthropic organizations and private schools are a great place to look. Just be prepared to write a big check. Rounds at Winged Foot can go for as high as $2,000 a player.

Be a Volunteer

What Augusta's elite members will never tell you is that there really is a way to get onto the course: Become a volunteer. Next time you're watching the Masters, keep an eye open for all the gray-haired men carrying QUIET signs. These are gallery guards. Becoming a gallery guard is not easy. But it's also not impossible. For years, a friend of mine has sent his best clients to work as gallery guards. Beginning Sunday before the Masters and lasting through the final round, they arrive at the course around sunrise and work until sunset. Then several weeks after the tournament, they all come back for a day at the course, when they'll get to play. Augusta will deny this, but it is true.

Hang Out with Sales Guys and Insurance Agents

Yes, I know the old Woody Allen joke about trying to commit suicide by inhaling next to an insurance salesman. But these guys know their golf. And they know how to get onto golf courses. Pine Valley and Merion are frequent sites for sales outings.

Don't Ask

The surest way to never get invited anywhere is to ask. Asking to play is considered to be in bad taste.

Don't Bribe

This might sound obvious, but you'd be surprised how many people try to buy their way onto top courses. This strategy might work, but it's more likely to lead to great embarrassment. In 2001, Pine Valley expelled two members who had been selling off tee times at $7,500 a player. Not long before, Augusta suspected a member for taking "sweeteners" from guests. Augusta also reportedly forced two other members to resign after another member discovered the pair were charging guests $10,000 a round.

And, just so you don't forget, make sure to always check your voice mail.

Golf is about
seeking perfection

Charles Schwab is an icon of financial services—the man most recognized for bringing Wall Street to Main Street. He's also an avid golfer and has used business savvy and a love of the sport to become one of golf's most prominent figures. His company sponsors both the PGA and Senior PGA Tours and the senior circuit's $1 million Charles Schwab Cup.

"Golf has a very clear set of rules that everyone plays by. It is global. I never get tired of it. It's a lot like life: You never get perfection. Tom Kite just shot 67 playing with me, and afterward I said, 'Tom, what are you going to do?' He said, 'I'm going to practice. I've got some things to work on.' It's the same with business. You never completely satisfy your customer. Innovation must be unrelenting. If you don't keep working, you go out of business."

LESSON 5

Keep your eye on the ball (most of the time).

Meet the Ron Popeil
of Golf

REMEMBER THOSE ADS for Remington rechargeable shavers in which Victor Kiam coined the phrase "I liked it so much, I bought the company."? That would pretty much sum up the career of Rob O'Loughlin. Now O'Loughlin is no household name—far from it. In the pantheon of famous CEOs, he's nonexistent. But just because he hasn't been on the cover of *Forbes* doesn't mean you shouldn't listen to his story. In fact, what you'll find from this smooth-talking Texan is that he's been able to perfectly blend a passion for golf into his business life to the point that it is impossible to spot where golf ends and business begins. As O'Loughlin told me, "Golf and business are the same for me."

The story of how Rob O'Loughlin found his own piece of greatness began on a wet day in 1994 at the Muirfield Village Golf Club in Dublin, Ohio. O'Loughlin was modestly successful at the time. He was the owner of a thriving chain of tuxedo rental businesses and the previous part-owner of two professional basketball teams. He was the type of guy who believed that the golf course was the best place to conduct business and the best place to come up with new business ideas.

What happened that day went like this: It had been raining for several days and the course was muddy. Shortly before O'Loughlin and his group teed off, the pro instructed each player to take off his shoes so that their traditional metal cleats could be replaced with a new plastic cleat that would not tear up the waterlogged greens. O'Loughlin complained that he didn't drag his feet when he played. But the pro informed him that the order had come down from Jack Nicklaus himself. And since the Golden Bear ran the course, players had to do what he said.

So O'Loughlin tossed his metal cleats and went out to play. After a few holes, he noticed that the plastic cleats were lighter and gripped the ground just fine. By the eighteenth hole, he decided to call up the company that made them and buy a few boxes for his buddies back home in Madison, Wisconsin. But when he made that call, the salesman who answered told him that the plastic cleats could only be sold to golf courses. O'Loughlin said he would be happy to introduce the cleats to one of the private clubs where he belonged. The salesman again refused. "The boss doesn't want me to do that," he said. Never one to be shy and go away, O'Loughlin asked for the boss's phone number. A short time later, he bought the company, renamed it Softspikes and started revolutionizing the golf business. Nine years and one billion plastic cleats later, the company had grown annual sales from $200,000 to $32 million and O'Loughlin sold the business to a New York investment firm for a handsome payday. He and his partners—who included country singer Larry Gatlin and a former basketball pro turned fast-food maven named Junior Bridgeman—pocketed many times their initial investment.

This sort of thing doesn't happen to most of us, which is why we need to learn what O'Loughlin has to teach. I first met him several years ago through a mutual acquantaince. I liked him instantly. He's a great salesman because he is so easy to like. He's the type of person who can have a conversation with anyone. Mind you, he doesn't come across like a slick sales guy.

I caught up with O'Loughlin at Muirfield Village not long ago, where he had invited me and my father. Ostensibly, the reason was to tell me about his latest gadget, a handheld distance finder for golfers called the Laser Link QuickShot. O'Loughlin discovered Laser Link inadvertently while negotiating the acquisition of a company in Vancouver that used GPS technology to calculate distances between a golfer and the flagstick. During the negotiations, a struggling inventor in Minneapolis happened to call O'Loughlin and tell him about his product. The device copied the way lasers are used in real estate, as well as by hunters and the military, to measure distances and was far simpler than the satellite system required for GPS. O'Loughlin loved the idea. He soon bought the company from the inventor.

The catch was that Laser Link, like all distance finders, was illegal for use by professional golfers. That actually was the business opportunity. O'Loughlin knew he had a great product; he then needed to create a market. And that meant convincing the most powerful forces in golf to change the rules.

When we arrived, O'Loughlin was waiting for us outside our guest cottage. He was charming from the start—just the right mix of familiarity and friendliness while maintaining respect. It was too late for golf, so we ventured over to the dining room, a room with tall windows overlooking the eighteenth green. O'Loughlin launched into a story about a trip he had made just the week before to St. Andrews where he met with Peter Dawson, the legendary secretary of the Royal & Ancient Golf Club. He had gone over to the fabled home of golf to lobby Dawson and his club to approve the use of Laser Link and other range finders. "We laughed and he didn't agree with me one bit," said O'Loughlin. "Peter's idea was that change should not happen quickly. Me, I'm a change agent. I told Peter, there are more golf courses in Alabama than in Scotland. I just wanted to make the point. He's got all the power, but he'll see it my way. Eventually."

O'Loughlin had us in stitches all evening with his stories. He was a repository for facts about his businesses. The son-in-law of cable TV pioneer Jim Fitzgerald, he'd been part-owner of both the Milwaukee Bucks and the Golden State Warriors. He'd rented 3 million tuxedos. ("That's a whole lot of weddings.") He'd sold 1 billion plastic cleats. ("Make 'em for a nickel, sell 'em for a quarter.") He'd convinced 1,200 golf courses to install tiny prisms on every flagstick so that a laser beam could then calculate distances. ("It's the simplest thing in the world.") But he was not pushy or obnoxious. He didn't so much brag as poke fun at himself and his insatiable exuberance. He joked that because he'd grown up in Texas the son of a doctor and a nurse and the fifth of seven siblings, he'd learned to stand his ground. "My wife sometimes reminds me of the motto on my family coat of arms," he said in his mix of Texas twang and Midwestern cadence. "Often wrong, seldom in doubt."

The next morning, we came together on the practice range. After warming up with a few wedges, O'Loughlin started his pitch. He presented me with a gold-colored Laser Link device, which looked sort of like a phaser from *Star Trek*. He had me point the device at a distant flagstick and hold my finger down on a button. A second later, the number 196 appeared on a screen telling me the yardage. "Now point it at me," he said. I did and learned that he was five yards away. He then engaged in a competition with our caddie, seeing who could point and click the fastest and get the right distance.

Later, on number 11, he watched me hit a 3 wood as well as I ever have only to see it land in the water. He pointed his Quick-Shot from where I stood and clicked. "We're 270 yards to the pin," he told me. "In 1997, Tiger was right where you are and hit a 2 iron against the pin and sank the Eagle," the suggestion being that I had the wrong club and that I certainly wasn't Tiger.

I can't remember a moment of the round when O'Loughlin *wasn't* talking. At one point, he had hit his ball into the woods and ventured off with the caddy. There he was, kneeling under a thick branch, explaining to the caddy how to use the Laser Link from any part of the course. He then smacked his shot out of danger and just short of the green, from where he got up and down for par.

So what did I learn from O'Loughlin? Several things.

1. Listen.

As much as he talked, he listened. He has a great ability to soak in what people tell him. Where this plays a role in his professional life is that listening allows him to understand what troubles people and what would make their lives easier.

2. Take what you hear and find solutions.

How many times have you been stuck in a slow round of golf and then been further annoyed while the players in front wander around searching for yardage markers on elusive sprinker heads? O'Loughlin reckoned that he could reduce slow play and help people become more accurate.

3. Keep it simple.

"There's a lot of stuff right under our noses that people don't think of," O'Loughlin explained. "There's a lot of people in Silicon Valley thinking of all these complex things, but I look for what is simple. I look for TV remote controls and garage door openers that are simple to understand and really make people's lives better."

4. Don't be a typical salesman.

This might sound odd coming from a guy who is the consumate salesman. However, O'Loughlin himself believes that not very many salesmen are worth listening to. "I remember in college, there was one thing I knew I didn't want to be and that was a salesman," he explained. "My notion of a salesman was a guy who graduated last year and came back and wanted to talk to you about insurance and you ran the other way. But what I learned is that selling is the best job there is as long as you believe in what you are selling. I see myself as on a mission to help people. That's the way I view my businesses. My specialty is that I'm in the change business. I'm not selling cars. I'm selling something to guys who never imagined needing a Laser Link and showing them how it will make it easier for them to play golf."

5. Get people to like you.

O'Loughlin learned early on that the key was getting people to like him. "A guy told me early in my career that you don't sell the product, you sell yourself first," he said. "It's like when you go into a store and you really don't want to buy those shoes but you like the salesman so much that you do it anyway."

6. Don't be afraid to mix business and golf.

O'Loughlin does almost all his business on the golf course and says that before he hires a new employee he takes him golfing to get to know him better. He does the same with customers. That way, he can let them test the product without having to endure a dull presentation of laser technology. Such efforts led to both Jack Nicklaus and Arnold Palmer discovering the Laser Link device and lending their endorsements. On one occasion, O'Loughlin's father-in-law presented a device to George H. W. Bush, who used it during a round with his son George W. in Kennebunkport, Maine. The two Bushes were photographed using the device by the *New York Times*.

How did all this turn out for O'Loughlin? Not long after we played golf, O'Loughlin sent me an e-mail saying that Peter Dawson and the R&A had approved the use of Laser Link by professionals in an amended rule. He was already ramping up production to meet the demand he insisted would follow. I asked him how it was going and he told me he was selling Laser Links as fast as he could make them. Other competitors like Bushnell were also benefitting from the ruling. But O'Loughlin was clearly the victor, having spent the better part of five years lobbying for a change.

So what was he doing now? Still selling. Still delivering the softest hard sell you've ever heard. "I've got to go," he said in a hurry. "I'm on the board of the local bank and I'm going out golfing with the president of the bank and a big construction guy in town who we want to bank with us. We'll go out, have lunch, play golf. We'll hit some good shots and some bad shots. We'll have a drink afterwards. He won't feel like we were making a sales call. And he'll get to see Laser Link at work."

LESSON 6

Don't be afraid to imagine.

Rembrandt with an
Earth Mover

I **F YOU SURVEYED GOLFERS** about their favorite course architects, you'd likely hear an assortment of names from Tillinghast
and Ross to Dye and Nicklaus. My vote would go to Tom
Fazio. Fazio is as close to an artist as you will ever meet on a golf
course. He believes in challenging a player, but also making the
experience memorable with lush colors and dramatic vistas. For
those reasons, he is also the most sought-after architect among the
wealthiest developers in the world. Casino impresario Steve Wynn
spent $60 million for Fazio to turn his piece of the Las Vegas
desert into a lush oasis now known as Shadow Creek. The members of Augusta National recruited him to toughen up their own
course and restore its beauty.

What also makes Fazio so sought after is that he is hard to get.
In the 1990s, for instance, a group of Japanese businessmen approached him to build a course in a country several oceans away

from his beloved North Carolina mountains. Fazio, who has designed more than 200 courses in the United States since 1963,
was reluctant. This is a man who can't abide the room-service life
and rarely ventures more than 800 miles—the approximate range
of his twin-engine turboprop—from his wife and six children in
sleepy Hendersonville.

The suitors, however, were the type that don't mind adding
zeros to a paycheck, so they kept asking and Fazio kept politely
turning them down. One day they marched down Main Street in
Hendersonville to make yet another offer. When they got to the
architect's office, they came face to face with a handwritten sign
that asked, WHAT PART OF THE WORD "NO" DON'T YOU UNDER-
STAND? His answer to the foreign investors stood. In fact, he
stubbornly refuses to build more than six courses a year, does
much of his own legwork, and avoids such gimmicks as "signa-
ture" holes whose inclusion on a course too often appear at the
neglect of the other seventeen. Ask anyone who has played a
Fazio course: Each hole is framed as a distinct, original portrait—
using a palette that includes all the natural elements—while en-
suring that golfers will be made to gulp hard as they stand on a
tee and prepare to play.

This is the Fazio I went to visit at Pinehurst, the century-old
golf resort located between Charlotte and Raleigh. Fazio had
built a new course on the remains of an old Donald Ross design.
Known as Pinehurst No. 4, it surrounds Ross's No. 2, host to
numerous major championships, including the 1999 U.S. Open,
which Payne Stewart won shortly before his tragic death, and the
2005 U.S. Open. In certain respects, No. 4 is a tribute to Ross—
with its unflinching demand for accurate, creative shot-making—
but with an added dose of beauty (huge stretches of sand, water,
and fairways look as if they were carved out of the earth). To my
mind, No. 4 is the prettier, more charming sister of No. 2,

though golfers hung up on the lore of No. 2 might consider such a description blasphemy since No. 4 has so rich a history.

I had convinced Fazio to join me for a round of golf at No. 4. We shared a bag of rental clubs. Fazio, who is now in his early sixties and wears thick glasses, plays the way Burt Bacharach sings— he knows the right notes but admits his specialty is the writing, not the performing (an aching neck makes the game even more challenging). We soon found ourselves standing on a fairway facing a daunting side-hill shot over two sets of pure white bunkers to an elevated green 160 yards away.

Fazio wanted to make me his guinea pig. Swinging a 6 iron with all my might, I sent the ball soaring toward the hole, just left of the flag, and watched with disappointment as it buried in the trap. Fazio smirked. "You didn't think," he said, handing me an 8 iron for a mulligan. "If you want to play my courses well, you have to use your mind. Now hit this one straight at the hole and let the landing area in front of the green do the work for you."

"I can't hit an 8 that far."

"Just try it."

I played my shot, doubting that the ball would make it within 30 yards of the target. A few seconds later, having bounced and rolled its way through certain danger, my ball rested on the edge of the green 30 feet from the hole. "Get the idea?" he said with a chuckle.

Fazio insisted that every hole should be playable and every error correctable for those with imagination. He demonstrated this from a spot several yards to the side of the first hole, a 338-yard par-4. (We backtracked because Fazio rarely likes to tour a course in its numeric order. He gets bored with the chronology of the scorecard and likes to imagine his own courses within the existing eighteen holes.) After dropping several balls to a position at the bottom of a rolloff 30 feet below the pin, he took a pitching wedge—the typical choice—and landed the ball within 15 feet of the cup. It rested there a moment, then gathered pace and rolled past the cup before careening off the far end of the green into a waiting pot bunker. Not the thinking shot, he said. Then, with a 4 iron, he smacked a second ball into the side of the mound before the green, and it skipped up to the hole and stopped within a foot. The thinking shot.

Fazio said his goal is to scare every player but not make them flee the course. He accomplishes this with pot bunkers, for example, that provide direction (as in, "Stay away from this side of the fairway unless you're really good.") as well as add color and texture to the fairway. Pine trees are sometimes moved to open space for light and shadow much like a painter might use shading. And flowers often highlight the land above a green and behind the tee boxes.

In certain respects, Fazio is also like the conductor of an orchestra. Opening holes are dotted with flowers and pot bunkers—reminiscent of Scottish links golf but harmless to the well-struck ball. By the par-4 seventh, we're forced to navigate around a waste bunker that runs the entire 410 yards of the hole. From there, more sand and elevations require us to recalibrate our distances—hitting a 5 iron from 200 yards on one hole and from 120 yards a few holes later. The crescendo builds to the closing hole, an uphill 400-yard par-4, where a tee shot looks out at the old clubhouse and, as on the first tee, reminds us that Bobby Jones, Ben Hogan, and Jack Nicklaus all walked Pinehurst. The hole is dramatic but fair.

I started waxing on about the history when he stopped me in my tracks. "Golf writers won't ever admit this," he told me, "but it's just a game. It's not surgery or nuclear science. I'm supposed to let people have fun."

With that, he called to three of his designing cohorts, who have been playing a round as he and I tour the course. "Okay, guys, closest to the hole for a buck," he said. "I get two, you guys get one, because I'm the boss." A course ranger came over to inform us that we shouldn't be goofing around on the greens but disappeared upon noticing Fazio. One by one, each of us attempted a shot from 50 yards over deep sand traps to a pin cut close to the edge of the green with a steep decline beyond it. Nearly impossible. Fazio stuck his six feet from the pin, arguably even with his longtime assistant Blake Bickford. When it was my turn, Fazio pulled $10 out of his wallet and announced he was upping the ante. Shortly after, having refused to take my money, he was hurrying to the nearby airport to get back to Hendersonville in time to watch his daughter play soccer.

"Remember," he coached, "I want people to feel that the hole they're playing is something they like, so that they won't use my name while cursing, and they'll think to themselves that at that moment this is the only place they want to be."

Fazio left after our final putts. As he walked away, I realized just how remarkable he seemed. He was so balanced in his appreciation of the game and so willing to be creative and learn. He was, I decided, Rembrandt with an earth mover.

Golf is about multitasking

Bill Foley is the chairman and CEO of Fidelity National Financial, the country's largest title-insurance and real-estate services company. He's also the founder and managing director of Foley Estates Vineyard & Winery and, until recently, served as chairman of CKE Restaurants, parent company of Hardee's and Carl's Jr. He remains a single-digit handicapper with a terrific short game. When I asked him how he maintains an impressive handicap while running two major corporations and a booming winery he told me:

"I've been that way since I was at West Point. The academy taught me about organization and delegating and still paying attention to detail. After the service, I got a law degree, practiced full-time for eight or nine years, and then started dabbling in business investing. I had an opportunity in 1984 to buy a small title-insurance company, which was Fidelity National. I put together a group of guys and we did a leveraged buyout. We watched every dollar. Ten years later I put together a group to buy a controlling interest in Carl's Jr. and then Hardee's. The winery was just something on the side, but it's become a success."

LESSON 7

Be yourself.

Minding Your Manners

I'M OFTEN ASKED, "How should I behave when I'm playing golf at a really top club?" Now I'm no Mr. Manners—just ask my wife, who has endured years of badly timed jokes and more feet in my mouth than there are on a centipede's left side. But I've experienced a few rarified moments like the lobster appetizer at the National Golf Links while overlooking Peconic Bay, the pressure of standing on the first tee at Pebble Beach where a few dozen tourists congregate to comment on your swing, and old-fashioned customs like relaxing in the bar after a round at Winged Foot. And so I've learned an important lesson: You can be the worst golfer in the world, but if you behave properly you will leave a positive impression. Conversely, if you act like a jerk it doesn't matter if you play with the skill of a pro. What matters in golf is acting like, well, a gentleman. How many times have you seen perfectly normal people act like total idiots on the golf course? Recently I played at a top track with a friend, and was teamed with two well-known investment bankers. Despite club rules forbidding the use of cell phones, one of the bankers kept answering his phone and conducting conversations. It got to the point where after he'd interrupted consecutive tee shots with his ring tone of *Beethoven's Fifth,* I walked up to him and declared, "Are you on the phone with President Bush? He must be seeking your advice on North Korea for the call to be this important."

Like I said, I'm no gentleman. But I'd like to be. Sort of.

A somewhat sarcastic yet brilliant editor of mine at *Fortune* named Erik Torkells once ran across an advertisement for a new program at the Gleneagles resort in Scotland offering to teach guests how to behave like gentlemen. Gleneagles is an 80-year-old oasis of luxury that has three top golf courses and extensive lands that are a playground for the wealthy and powerful. The package included lessons on choosing the right whiskey and cigars and working properly with a caddie in addition to assorted classes on hunting, shooting skeet, and falconry. I assumed that the target market was the 27-year-old Wall Streeters I'd seen ordering $1,200 bottles of wine at Le Bernardin but then splattering Châteaux Margaux on their Hermès ties. This was back in the days of the dot-com boom when money was filling the magazine's coffers and spending $800 a day for a writer to learn about how to live like a character from Masterpiece Theatre was a no-brainer. And so I flew off to the foothills of the Scottish Highlands and a week at Gleneagles to see if I could learn how to be that gentleman.

I have to admit to feeling uncomfortable as I drove my rented Ford up the driveway of Gleneagles. The place was teeming with prestige, having hosted presidents and prime ministers for decades. I had read that the hotel employed more than one employee per guest—a fact that does not necessarily mean impeccable service but guarantees you won't spend a lot of time in line. Indeed, as I stopped at the entrance, I was strangely alone. And then suddenly a giant of a man in a kilt came out to meet me and directed me to the front desk.

Soon after, I decided to pay my first of many visits to the hotel's wood-paneled, cigar-scented bar called The Bar. I requested a glass of Scotch and the bartender quickly explained that they didn't have anything called "Scotch." What they had was whiskey—and a lot of it. "We have more than 200 whiskeys, from under 20 pounds a glass to more than 300 pounds. We just had some fellows from UBS come in and spend $7,000 on a bottle of 40-year-old." Okay, I responded, perhaps something a bit more economical. Which one should I try? "Have you had dinner yet, sir?" The implication being that the strength of whiskey he poured me would depend on my ability to drink on an empty stomach. Since I hadn't yet eaten, he kindly served me what had to be whiskey's alternative to a Shirley Temple. He would save the powerful stuff for the next night.

The next afternoon, my shooting instructor met me in the hotel lobby and drove us across the road to the Jackie Stewart Shooting School. (Yes, that Jackie Stewart.) In khakis, polo shirt, and a blue V-neck sweater, I felt distinctly out of place next to the barrel-chested man in knickers and high leather boots as he handed me a double-barreled Beretta and told me to aim at the clay pigeon that would shortly fly into the air.

"Almost got that one, sir!" my instructor heartily informed me after each miss. It's nice being called "sir," especially when you keep missing the target. Suddenly the pigeon soared, I pulled the trigger, and the pigeon exploded. "Got it, sir!"

I started feeling like being a gentleman meant sticking to a tight schedule. Shortly after we finished shooting, another guide appeared in a Range Rover to take me to the golf course. There, he introduced me to my caddy. It turned out we were playing as a single. I was, it seems, the only wanna-be gentleman at the resort participating in the package.

One of the most amazing things about Scotland is how quickly the weather can shift. I began my round on the King's Course in the sun with only a slight breeze. The King's Course, Gleneagles's gem, was designed in 1919 by five-time British Open champion James Braid. The course is a maze of blind tee shots (as well as rough, which seems to attract tee shots like magnets to a refrigerator). By the fourth hole, rain was sprinkling, but not enough for me to wish for an umbrella or put on a jacket— neither of which I had brought with me. At the seventh hole, the floodgates opened. After 30 seconds, my sweater had taken on five pounds of water.

We quickly finished the hole, then on the eighth tee asked the foursome ahead if we could play through. Three of the men said that would be fine. But the most vocal of the group refused to let us pass. When he knocked his ball 50 yards left of the fairway, we asked again to play through and got his begrudging approval.

"English, they were," said my Scottish caddy.

"Are the English usually rude?" I asked quietly.

"You've seen *Braveheart*? They're kind of like that."

We joined up with three Scots having a tough time in the rain. By now it was late. My hands, slippery and numb from two hours in a downpour, gripped a 9 iron as I took a stance in the foot-deep heather wrapped around my wayward golf ball. Swinging with all my might, I hit the ball 75 yards into a 20-mile-per-hour wind and it plopped into a deep bunker. It was the perfect time to blurt out an obscenity, right? Before I could, one of my playing partners offered a suggestion: "Up for a spot of tea?"

Minutes later we were in the cozy halfway house sipping Earl

Grey and nibbling warm bacon sandwiches—Irish bacon, which is salty and delicious, particularly when one is on the verge of hypothermia. I sat on a bench, wiping the water off my hair, and wondering how I was ever going to explain to my friends back at the office that this wasn't fun.

One of the local customs—known by all the local gentlemen— is that groups tee off on No. 11 and stop in for a brief cup of tea before completing the hole. This is something the Englishmen behind us could not tolerate, and as we returned to play, we noticed the *Braveheart* foursome had hit their shots, run in for tea, and then jumped in front of us. This was an affront to my partners. Englishman and Scotsman stand side to side, each with a short-iron in hand, each wondering who would relinquish and fall back. The two groups almost came to blows—literally. One of the Scotsmen lifted a fist and yelled, "You're no gentleman, sir!" The Englishman stood stunned, and we played on. Later, the Scotsman asked me what had brought me to his home turf.

"Funny as this might sound," I said, with rain still pouring over my face, "I'm here to learn about how to become a gentleman."

The Scotsman gave me a smile. "Well, my boy, let's get you a whiskey."

Three hours later I found myself in the Gleneagles wine cellar, surrounded by bottles of Dom Perignon and Château Margaux, with a glass of whiskey in my hand. The hotel's astute sommelier guided me around a selection of six classic malts, moving from the 14-year-old Oban, aged in kegs kept close to the sea, to double-mature deep-amber Lagavulin, to Glenmorangie, aged in old port kegs and slightly sweet. Between sips, we nibbled on bits of white chocolate. Later he brought in a whiskey aged in claret kegs that could easily have been used to start a barbecue. What I learned: Never inhale too close or you may burn your nostrils; swirl the whiskey like a glass of wine; and pay attention to where the whiskey comes from. Oh, and one more thing: Take smaller sips.

By the time I reached the dinner table in the Strathearn restaurant, my head was spinning. I'm a lightweight when it comes to liquor and I was clearly swooning from the whiskey. If that wasn't enough to put a smile on my face, I suddenly noticed that the restaurant itself was one of the most glamorous I had ever seen. It actually looked like the dining room on the *Titanic*, which I'm told was its model. You walk through giant doors into a blindingly white hall with tables spread far apart, some near a piano, which pumps out a steady flow of Cole Porter tunes, others back near windows overlooking the lawns. Waiters are dressed in tuxedos, hair slicked back. It was all formal enough to make me tighten the knot in my tie and stand up straighter.

Without asking, the kindly sommelier came along with an exceptionally dry 1994 Chablis grand cru to start my meal. I had always thought of Chablis as the pinkish stuff that Orson Welles used to plug in TV commercials. But this was no Paul Mason. It was dazzlingly crisp. I made a note about the flavor and finished off the glass with a plate of smoked salmon. Then came the main course. I had ordered venison tenderloin in plum sauce. A pair of waiters presented it to me under a silver cover, which they lifted with not the least hint of smiles. To heighten the experience, the friendly sommelier once again appeared, now with an aged Volnay, a syrupy red Burgundy. I was trying my hardest to keep the wine from going to my head. And in fact it might have had a slow time getting there because of the logjam created by the whiskey. Though I really wanted to act like a gentleman, I found my chin becoming part of my neck. For a moment, I lightly hummed the Bobby Darin tune being played on the piano. In the blur before me, I watched the busboy remove my finished plate and the sommelier once again approach me.

"Would you like dessert, sir?"

"I think I'm pretty full," I answered.

"Well, then, how about some special cheeses with a glass of . . . (Don't say it! Don't say it!) . . . port." There, he had said it. I couldn't resist port, particularly not when it was a Dow's 1977. Even I knew that Dow's 77 is one of the four or five best years ever for port. So I did the only thing an inebriated writer with an expense account would do. Against all the little warnings in my head about having already consumed eight other varieties of alcohol, I ordered a glass. Half an hour later, when I floated out of the restaurant and all the servers wished me a good night, I congratulated myself for remaining a gentleman and not showing my state of drunkenness. Even in the middle of the night, when the room was spinning and I found myself promising God I would never make this mistake again if only he would help me survive this one time, I was proud of myself.

The next thing I remember was the phone ringing. It was late morning and my instructor was waiting in the lobby to take me hunting for the afternoon. I threw on some clothes and ran down to the breakfast room. I took one look at the traditional Scottish breakfast—which consisted of foods I don't traditionally eat like Loch Fyne kippers, haggis, and black pudding—and opted to go forward on an empty stomach.

We weren't just going hunting. We were going hawking. The resort, home to the fabled British School of Falconry, had arranged for a guide to take me into the woods in search of rabbits. By the time we got to the school, sunshine had turned to icy rain. I kept thinking that this was some sort of a joke, that we weren't seriously going hunting with birds instead of guns. In truth, I'd never hunted for anything in my life except the occasional wayward golf ball. But there they were, these enormous hawks waiting for us. After some preliminary training in how to make a bird sit on my arm, fly off, and return, we marched into the woods with two of the more ferocious-looking hawks. The one on my arm was named French. My guide described French as a killing machine and said she hadn't been fed in a while.

Hawking works like this: You send the bird up into the trees where she can more easily search for prey. Then you stomp around the forest trying to scare up rabbits. We hadn't been hunting for 10 minutes when a rabbit jumped in front of me, and French rocketed down and clutched it with her talons. My guide jumped into the scrap, pulled the rabbit from French, and handed me a chicken head to feed to French. We literally pulled this hungry, flesh-eating bird away from its kill. I kept wondering how stupid this seemed. But we repeated this routine three times until the rain became unbearable.

It was at this point that I learned the true measure of a gentleman. The magazine wanted some pictures of me doing all the gentlemanly things I had learned. The photographer decided he wanted a picture of French landing on my arm. That required first sending French up into a tree, then showing off a piece of chicken in my gloved hand in order to get French's attention. At the sight of the chicken, French flew with wings outstretched toward me and landed on my arm while simultaneously snatching the chicken from my hand. The problem was that when a large predator is flying toward you it is awfully hard not to blink. This annoyed the photographer to no end. In take after take, I flinched as French's talons passed my face. I have to admit to being kind of nervous, particularly after the photographer yelled at me. Finally, I decided to think like a gentleman. I took a deep breath, held out my hand for French, and when she landed, without blinking, I leaned forward and gave her a big kiss on the beak.

So what did this experience at Gleneagles teach me? The truth is that I felt like a phony. It's not that I didn't appreciate all the whiskey and the great golf. Heck, that venison dinner was one of the best meals I've ever had. But I didn't feel like myself. I felt like I was trying to be someone else. And in that is the greatest lesson. I often see people trying to be something they aren't. At dinner just the other night, I listened to two young men going on and on about expensive wines and their favorite cigars. But they kept mispronouncing the names of the wines. The truth is that being a gentleman has nothing to do with the kind of food you order or cigars you smoke. How many obnoxious fat guys have blown cigar smoke in your direction?

In the end, I've learned three lessons. One is that you should act naturally wherever you are playing golf and with whomever you are playing. If affectations impress them, then they probably aren't right for you anyway. The second is that common courtesy is the true measure of a gentleman—something the friendly Scotsman showed me on that rainy afternoon. And the third? Never drink whiskey on an empty stomach.

LESSON 8

Keep your enemies close.

The "King" of Golf

ON ONE OF THOSE GENTLE, Southern California after-noons, Mark King was waiting for me on the first tee at La Costa. King is the CEO of TaylorMade-adidas Golf, one of the world's leading clubmakers. For a man who was a football, basketball, and baseball standout in high school, he is relatively small in stature, but he has a booming personality, which makes him seem much larger. He has a smile full of white teeth, a golden tan, and one of those George Clooney hairstyles from the mid-1990s. He is an unabashed flirt and could charm the dourest skeptic.

Like most rounds, we didn't begin by discussing much more than the weather and playing conditions. The course was kind of soggy and looked like a sickly cousin of the championship layout that hosts the Accenture World Match Play Championship each year. King talked about how much he liked Spaniard Sergio Garcia (who endorses TaylorMade) and his family. He mentioned he'd been negotiating a contract with Greg Norman but the talks had gone nowhere. We hit some shots and told jokes. Then, when he seemed comfortable, I began to ask him about himself.

Although I'd known King for a number of years, I'd never been with him outside his office. What interested me was that he'd spent his entire professional career at TaylorMade. He'd started a few years after the company introduced the first metal-woods in 1979—a product launch that began the era of ever longer tee shots. He'd risen from sales rep to CEO but the ride wasn't without bumps. It was how he overcame the rough times, dueled with Callaway Golf, and returned TaylorMade to the top of the golf business that caught my interest. When I approached him about meeting on the golf course, he was initially reluctant. He said he was afraid he'd say something stupid. Quite the contrary, he ended up being an enlightening, informed, and even inspirational interview. But before we get there, you need to step back and understand the relationship between Taylor-Made and Callaway.

The thing about golf is that it isn't a growing sport. Despite the popularity of Tiger Woods and masses of new faces in tournament galleries, the number of golfers has been stagnant for years. Those of us who are worried about not getting a tee time because the course is too crowded might see that as good news. Not to people who are in the business of making and selling golf clubs. Because the pie isn't growing, every dollar in revenue that one manufacturer takes in is a dollar another has lost. That creates a certain kill-or-be-killed mentality. This would be the case in almost any industry. But in golf, what's made the rivalries even more intense is that most of the major manufacturers are located in tiny Carlsbad, California—not much more than a few solid tee shots from one another. TaylorMade and Callaway actually share an office park. The result of their proximity is that these two companies hate each other.

I got to see these rivalries up close one evening at a local watering hole. Several thousand white guys in khakis and golf shirts had just ended the workday at the dozens of golf-equipment companies—clubmakers, ballmakers, shaftmakers—housed in sterile office parks in the area. A few dozen had just arrived at the Karl Strauss brewpub. At one end of the restaurant were four men who worked for TaylorMade. I knew that because each wore a golf shirt bearing the company's logo. I introduced myself and asked if I could sit down. Other tables were filled with men wearing shirts emblazoned with the names Titleist, Cobra, or Aldila. No one seemed to mind the proximity until two men dressed in Callaway shirts entered the restaurant. As they passed the Taylor-Made table, the two Callaway men looked over and nodded. No one smiled. Finally one of the TaylorMade men leaned over to me and said, "They don't speak to us, and we don't speak to them."

Location is about all TaylorMade and Callaway have in common. To Callaway, free-wheeling TaylorMade is "the Frat House." TaylorMade mocks its insular rival as "the Firm." Callaway traditionally made clubs for average golfers, while TaylorMade took the clubs pro golfers were using and adjusted them to suit amateurs. Callaway focuses on management and production efficiency while sticking to core product designs, much the way Ford built cars around a basic chassis. TaylorMade, run by sales guys, is constantly reinventing its product lines. Callaway compells its employees to wear jackets and ties. TaylorMade's people dress like golfers.

Even on an executive level, the two seem like opposites. Callaway execs belong to the haughty Del Mar Country Club. TaylorMade people join the less impressive Shadow Ridge Country Club. They live in different neighborhoods; TaylorMade people tend to bunch up around middle-class Vista, while Callaway's executives often prefer tonier Del Mar and Rancho Santa Fe. Their kids go to different schools. They have entirely separate social circles. In a town of just 78,000 residents, they hardly see one another. On the rare occasions they do, tensions often flare. A TaylorMade executive recalls being invited to a party a few years back at the house of a friend who had gone to work at Callaway. The executive and his wife stood around uncomfortably for a time with no one but their host speaking to them. One guest finally informed the executive and his wife that Callaway people did not socialize with TaylorMade people.

Ely Callaway probably would have wanted it that way. The charming Georgia-born salesman, who died in 2001, was an intense competitor with a masterful touch for building businesses. He did it in textiles in the 1960s, then as a vintner in the 1970s. Callaway came to Carlsbad in 1985 with the goal of creating a professionally run golf-club maker. He despised the status quo in town: the friendly golf matches between competitors, the haphazard approach to manufacturing, and the fact that most clubmakers cared only about satisfying skilled golfers. Hackers were an afterthought. Callaway's greatest contribution was recognizing that the high-handicap weekend player would spend big bucks for a club that was easy to hit.

The same could not be said of Gary Adams. Fun-loving, creative, and a tad eccentric, the Illinois native had started TaylorMade in 1979 and moved to Carlsbad a few years later. He became known as the father of the metalwood for developing the first metal-headed drivers, which soon replaced traditional persimmon heads. Like many visionaries he was an awful business manager. By the mid-1980s, Adams's financial shortcomings had brought TaylorMade to the edge of bankruptcy, and he was forced to sell to the French company Salomon.

TaylorMade entered a decade of declining sales and market

share, exacerbated by the 1991 launch of Callaway's Big Bertha driver. Big Bertha was a phenomenon: Annual sales hit $300 million within the first three years. As it turned out, pro golfers liked the club, too—and Tour validation is essential to marketing clubs. By 1998, Callaway, which had had almost zero presence on the pro tour before 1991, had two-thirds of the top pros using its clubs—and it wasn't even paying most of them to do so. That was no small accomplishment. The "driver count" calculated each week is golden among clubmakers because it lets the winner boast in ads that it has the No. 1 driver on the PGA Tour. And once the pros use your clubs, amateurs want them, too. Taylor-Made's share on tour sank from No. 1 to nearly nonexistent.

In 1997, Salomon merged with Adidas. The new parent overlooked TaylorMade's most spirited executive, Mark King. This would prove to be a pivotal error. King, who had gone to college on a golf scholarship and started as a sales rep for Taylor-Made in 1981, lived and breathed the golf business. He was also proud and more than a touch cocky. And so, spurned, he turned to the competition. Callaway hired him the next year to help start a golf-ball business. But King was out of sync at the company. A competitive scratch golfer, he loved being out on the course and schmoozing in Carlsbad. He was the exact opposite of his peers at Callaway, who might have loved golf just as much but rarely discussed the game. In fact, many were product guys who could have just as easily been selling cereal or laundry detergent. When the top spot at TaylorMade opened up 18 months later, King broke his employment contract with Callaway to grab it—even taking a pay cut—shortly before the golf-ball business officially launched. "I was offered a chance to come back and run a company where I had worked since college and where I had a family," says King. "The decision was a no-brainer."

An ugly legal dispute ensued when Callaway tried to prevent

King from going back to its competitor. At one point, Taylor-Made employees organized a King rally and hung a banner declaring FREE MARK KING from their headquarters building, visible to the many Callaway execs who drove past every day. Callaway has not forgotten the insult or the stunt. "It was like a top assistant coach quitting right before the Super Bowl to be head coach of the competition and taking the game plan with him," Callaway's top marketing executive, Larry Dorman, told me in a *Fortune* article. "That's what inflamed a lot of people."

No matter, Mark King was on his way to reinventing Taylor-Made.

"I wasn't a great student," Mark King said as we walked down a fairway. "I didn't go to a great school or get an MBA or get marketing training from Nike or Procter & Gamble. I think that because of what I *didn't* get I have an advantage, because I had to work harder than anyone else. I will outwork and out-try people. I don't let anything intimidate me. I am a very nervous person, whether that is taking a test or giving a presentation. But I jump in with both feet."

King needed to do just that with the resurrection of Taylor-Made. Upon his return, he drew up plans to rebuild the brand. Because golf is not a growing business, King had to find a way to take market share away from his competition. King knew he had to get extremely aggressive. He gutted the management team that had been running the company and then sat down his new team for intense discussions. "If I have a talent that helps me in this job," said King, "it's that I'm good at math. I spent three years studying math in college. What that taught me was problem solving and logical, sequential thinking. We sat down and asked basic questions. 'What do we have?' The answer was that we had basic products.

'What is our history?' We were known for making high-performance equipment for the best players. 'What had we become?' A company without a purpose. So we decided to go back to what we were. We jumped off a cliff without a parachute and figured we could learn how to fly before we hit the ground. We put all of our resources—I mean 100 percent—into reclaiming metalwood leadership. It wasn't being a genius. It was identifying the problems and solving them."

His strategy included a new line of woods and irons, an updated logo, and a more dogged sales force. He devised a three-tier line of clubs that targeted every level of golfer, from scratch players to duffers. He discarded TaylorMade's traditional copper-colored equipment, opting instead for a gunmetal blue similar to that of a sleek sports car. Problem was, TaylorMade had no credibility. At the August 2000 launch party for the new clubs, known as the 300 Series, only 5 of the 200 invited guests showed up. Twenty-four PGA Tour players were paid to use TaylorMade equipment, but only seven actually did. So King doubled the so-called tee-up money the company paid pros to use its clubs, from $500 a week to $1,000. He landed high-profile players such as the South African Ernie Els with generous annual contracts estimated to be in the seven-figure range. He also aggressively went after players who had no company allegiances by giving them prototypes of new clubs. The strategy worked: Within a few months the TaylorMade 300 was the hottest driver on tour. Less than a year later TaylorMade became the top seller of drivers among retailers despite being the priciest on the market at $399 for a driver.

Next, King unleashed an unprecedented product and marketing blitz. In an industry that expected product cycles to last 18 months or longer, King began releasing new drivers and irons in rapid-fire succession—the lower-cost 200 Series, the r500 Series, the larger-headed r5XD, the innovative r7 Quad. King was almost daring Callaway to match him club for club. Each new line had some kind of breakthrough, such as a lighter alloy or a wider sweet spot. And King had a flair for entertainment. While Callaway typically launched products with lengthy PowerPoint presentations, TaylorMade turned its launches into huge pep rallies. At the launch party for the r7 during the U.S. Open in 2004, for example, TaylorMade hired celebrity chef Todd English to prepare a seven-course meal for journalists, Tour players, and vendors. Spotlights spelled out the name of the club along the bottom of a swimming pool. Banners above waved the name. Everyone left with a bright red baseball cap with the TaylorMade logo and r7 in big letters. A similar event took place the week before the 2006 U.S. Open at Winged Foot for yet another product celebration. Dozens of reporters were invited to Trump National in Westchester County, New York, for a day of golf at The Donald's course. LPGA star Paula Creamer headlined the event with PGA Tour stars Sergio Garcia, Retief Goosen, and Fred Funk.

During the same period that King was working his magic Callaway was working on its own breakthrough driver, one that could hit the ball farther than any other club. There was just one little problem: It violated the rules of the U.S. Golf Association (USGA). Ely Callaway knew the club didn't conform, but in his stubborn confidence he told his people to go ahead anyway. He argued that it would be received with such gusto that the public would demand that the USGA change the rules.

Callaway introduced the ERCII driver in 2000. The USGA immediately labeled it illegal, stating that anyone who used the club would not be allowed to record a handicap. Sales flopped. Worse still, Callaway had no backup plan. And the company continued to struggle for more than two years—at one point deciding that smaller was better when the rest of the industry was making larger club heads that offered amateurs more margin for error. The move left the door open—and Mark King walked right through.

In the middle of it all, Ely Callaway became ill. After he had surgery in early 2001, doctors discovered a malignant tumor in his pancreas. He died in July 2001 at the age of 82. His successor, Ron Drapeau, named just months before Callaway's death, was almost immediately put on the defensive. In December 2001, Drapeau made the fateful decision to slash prices on Callaway's premium driver, the VFT Hawkeye, from $399 to $329 in order to undercut the pricy TaylorMade driver. It was a move that King had been waiting for. The price war had officially begun. The door swung open for TaylorMade to make a grab for market share. Before long, the two companies had switched positions. Now, instead of Callaway having the most PGA Tour players swinging its drivers, TaylorMade had the lead. More important, King had grown revenues at a double digit rate—more than 140 percent since he relaunched the company—versus an industry average that was in the low single digits.

I asked King what lessons he'd learned from the turnaround. He offered three. First was hard work. Second was the importance of surrounding himself with managers who shared his passion for the game. I've never met a group of people who love what they do as much as the designers and marketers at this company. The third lesson was that everyone in leadership should have a common commitment to the end goal. King then shared a fourth lesson gained from his observations of top golfers. The key to his company's success, he said, was that it "treated business like winning a major. You don't focus on winning when you start. You focus on being in the hunt on Sunday. We wanted to have a shot. When we got that shot, we went for it. But first we had to get in position. If we'd never done that, you wouldn't be talking to me. And I'd probably be unemployed."

That last idea has the most resonance with me. It says that success is about planning and being singularly focused on a goal but understanding that reaching that goal requires tremendous commitment.

Golf is about refusing to quit

Herb Kohler embodies the best of the Badger State. I've never met a more bullheaded man than this scion of the toilet industry. Yes, that Kohler—the one whose name is on almost every urinal and sink faucet from here to the Himalayas. But for all his success at flushing down waste, it is the waste that Kohler didn't flush that will be his greatest legacy. For more than a century, the Kohler family owned a swatch of land in Wisconsin that now contains the luxury American Club and several great courses including Whistling Straits.

Kohler and I caught up shortly before he was to host the 2004 PGA Championship. "I'm a hacker," Kohler confessed almost immediately. "I'm an 18-handicap trending toward 19. I play maybe fifty times a year—I played in Spain and Morocco just last week—but that hasn't improved my game much."

Do you have a favorite foursome?

The greatest time you'll ever have, is when I can get together with former President Bush, PGA Tour commissioner Tim Finchem, and Pete Dye. That's a hell of a game. Out of respect for the president, we play fast—but not too fast.

How'd you come to own one of the great golf destinations in the country?

continued

We had an old building that used to be a dormitory for European immigrants who worked at the company. My uncle built it in 1918. I cast around for what to do with it after it had long outlived its use. We decided on a village inn. You know, it took me three board meetings in a privately held company—of which I was CEO—to convince the board members to agree to my proposal. They couldn't imagine that an old-line manufacturer could do this.

We opened the hotel in 1981. In 1983 we decided to build a golf course. I contacted our VP of development, who happened to be a 2-handicap, and we went out and walked the land. Much of it was in wildlife zones and we didn't want to encroach on that. We finally picked a pair of designers and walked with them and talked about their philosophy and our philosophy. Then, in our inimitable wisdom, we fired them. I didn't find what they were doing interesting. We brought in Pete Dye in 1984. We were going to open in 1987, and we had just planted our greens and fairways in September 1986 when we had two 100-year floods within a week of one another. That totally wiped us out. We didn't open until 1988.

You are the third generation of Kohlers running the family business . . .

I know what you're going to say. I'm supposed to be the one who screws things up. I guess I haven't. We've gone from under $300 million when I became CEO in 1972 to about $3.5 billion today. That's primarily because

I absolutely love what we do. And we hire good people. We have a single level of quality whether we are making an engine, a piece of furniture, or a golf course. We try to live on the leading edge of design and technology. And then we maintain our drive by reinvesting 90 percent of our earnings back into the company.

LESSON 9

Be like the boss.

The Patron Saints of
Golf and Business

CEOS LOVE GOLF, obviously. One executive I know, Bill Kirkendall, left his job as CEO of Orlimar Golf to become a pro on the Champions Tour. He told me that being a pro was like running a small business but with the pressure of 10,000 people watching your every move. Others might not have turned professional but nonetheless play with an uncommon skill. In 2006, *Golf Digest* published its list of the 200 best golfing CEOs in the *Fortune* 1000. The top 10 listed with their handicap index were as follows:

> James Crane, Eagle Global Logistics (0.8)
> Jerry Jurgensen, Nationwide (0.9)
> Curt Culver, MGIC Investment (2.6)
> Theodore Chandler Jr., LandAmerica (3.0)
> John Lundgren, Stanley Works (3.0)

Stephen Macadam, BlueLinx Holdings (3.5)

Edward Stack, Dick's Sporting Goods (4.1)

Barry Davis, Crosstex Energy (4.2)

Stephen Bennett, Intuit (4.4)

Michael Eskew, UPS (5.2)

David Perdue, Dollar General (5.2)

Mayo Shattuck III, Constellation Energy (5.2)

The full list includes the most famous names in business. Charles Schwab ranks 42 with an 8 handicap index. The CEOs of McGraw-Hill, J. M. Smucker, Tyson Foods, McDonald's, Goodrich, Estee Lauder, Morgan Stanley, and Johnson & Johnson are all on the list. Over the years, being identified as a CEO who plays golf has fallen in and out of fashion. The rankings themselves seem to rise and fall with the performance of a company's stock, suggesting that someone like Scott McNealy of Sun Microsystems has enough time to rise to the top of the list when business is great; when things aren't so great, his game is certain to go downhill. But very clearly golf and CEOs are entwined. This relationship goes back more than 100 years to John D. Rockefeller.

Rockefeller is often cited as the patron saint of corporate golf. The founder of Standard Oil and, in his day, the wealthiest person in the world first picked up a golf club when he was nearly 60 years old while on vacation at a resort in 1899. He was instantly enamored with the game and played nearly every day for the remaining 33 years of his life. He even theorized that his quest to shoot par would enable him to live past 100.

Rockefeller was clearly addicted to the game. He built a golf course for his personal use at his estate in Tarrytown, New York, took instructions on the game, and even hired cameramen to film his swing so he could see for himself what he was doing right or wrong. His playing companions included Henry Ford, Harvey Firestone, and Andrew Carnegie but also Will Rogers. In his excellent book *Titan,* biographer Ron Chernow suggests that Rockefeller was equally passionate about two things: God and golf—and not necessarily in that order.

Despite his love of the game, I don't really agree with the popular notion that Rockefeller was the patron saint of corporate golf. He was neither the first business tycoon to take up the sport nor an advocate of golf as a tool for business. In fact, the expressly stated rule for teeing up with Rockefeller was that business not be a topic of discussion. The last thing Rockefeller wanted was to talk deals or be hit up for a loan. At the highest levels of business and golf, outright solicitation is still regarded as distasteful. But the connection between golf and business has evolved.

Though Rockefeller is largely seen as the patron saint, my vote is cast for a more modern figure: Jack Welch. Welch, for anyone who just returned to Earth from Mars, ran General Electric from 1981 until 2001 and is often considered to be the greatest corporate manager of the last 100 years. He was known as tough, brutally candid but also extremely passionate about identifying and developing new talent. One of the ways he did this was by playing golf. In an essay published in *Golf Digest,* Welch wrote that golf "is a sport that combines what I love: people and competition. The most enduring friendships of my life have been formed on and around the golf course."

Like Rockefeller, Welch did not grow up in an affluent household. His introduction to golf was as a caddy at Kernwood Country Club in Salem, Massachusetts. He taught himself the game starting at age nine and later was co-captain of his high school team and had a one-year stint on his college team.

But while his passion was golf, his gift was in leading a business. Starting in the early 1960s, he rose through the ranks at GE.

When he became CEO in 1981, GE was already known as a "golf company." Reginald Jones, who was CEO before Welch, was also an avid player and GE management meetings usually involved a round or two. However, Welch kicked it up a notch. Golf became an essential tool for any manager looking to move up. A friend of mine who worked at GE while Welch was there had never touched a club at the time he was hired. Soon after, his boss instructed him to buy a set of clubs and take lessons if he wanted a future at the company. The idea was not so much about schmoozing as it was the idea that golf was a litmus test for character. It showed whether a person had the guts to work in Welch's GE.

Welch made golf and business an acceptable, indeed encouraged, connection. He took the game from being a refuge for insurance agents and bankers and made it essential for all sorts of line managers. Annual management excursions to Augusta National became customary under Welch, enabling him to get to know his team. He kept memberships at a variety of clubs from Connecticut to Nantucket. He played far in excess of 50 rounds a year during his tenure, often in the company of senior managers but also with notables such as Bill Gates and Warren Buffett. Welch was as competitive on the course as off. When he was cited as the number-two golfer in the *Fortune* 500 behind Scott McNealy of Sun Microsystems, he engaged McNealy in a "friendly" match that lasted 36 holes. Welch won.

Perhaps his greatest golf course moment came in 1998. Playing at the Floridian, Wayne Huizenga's personal playground, Welch was with Huizenga, Matt Lauer from the *Today Show,* Bob Wright, who runs NBC, and Greg Norman. Norman shot two-under par-70 from the professional tees. Welch recorded a 69 from the shorter tees but made a point of telling everyone he met that he'd beaten the number-one player in the world. Norman later disputed this on national television. But Welch kept the scorecard in his office.

"If I had my preference," Welch once told *Business Week*, "I would have loved to have been a great professional golfer."

Welch might have wanted to be a touring pro, but the PGA Tour player you're about to meet in the next chapter would like to switch hats with Welch.

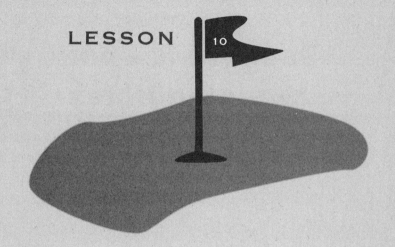

LESSON 10

Success is about the intangibles.

What Tiger and Buffett Have in Common

THE CRISP SOUND of 5 irons being launched into the sky resonated through the gallery. It was a Thursday morning in June, the start of the Barclays Classic at Westchester Country Club outside New York City. At opposite ends of the golf course were Phil Mickelson and Vijay Singh. On the practice range, preparing to start his round, Joe Ogilvie was working on his mid-irons, which hadn't been as consistent as he liked.

At 32, Ogilvie is a rising star on the PGA Tour. What's remarkable about Ogilvie is that he's able to navigate smoothly between the worlds of golf and business. Ogilvie loves business. From an early age he played in a foursome with his father and other local businesspeople in Lancaster, Ohio. As a teenager, he invested his lawn mowing earnings in a certificate of deposit and later dabbled in stocks. He went on to study economics at Duke

University. Then as a rising pro golfer, he was befriended by Warren Buffett after the newspaper in Omaha, Buffett's hometown, quoted Ogilvie saying that the famed investor was his hero. Ogilvie's relationship with Buffett and other businesspeople would prove pivotal in teaching him valuable lessons about how to succeed in golf.

Things have not come easily for Ogilvie, though he's had far more success than most on the Tour. After a stellar career on the Nationwide Tour, which included four victories, he recorded two second-place finishes in 2005, nearly winning the Bob Hope Chrysler Classic. But then he struggled through the first half of the 2006 season. Entering the Barclays, Ogilvie had missed the cut at the Players Championship and the Masters and then failed to qualify for the U.S. Open. His best finish had been a tie for twelfth at the FBR Open in Phoenix. But he'd also had some highlights, like his blistering 62 in the second round of the Byron Nelson Classic.

He was wondering how long the slump would last when I caught up with him around the time he was preparing for the Barclays. Ogilvie is one of the most well-spoken players on the Tour. He's thoughtful and intelligent. He explained to me how he took all the ups and downs as lessons to be learned. One of the reasons for his patience was that he'd had the benefit of exposure to some of the best minds in business. As a player, he'd taken advantage of pro-ams that often team Tour players with prominent businesspeople. He'd spent time with Jerry Jurgensen, the CEO of Nationwide, and Seth Waugh, who runs Deutsche Bank. Waugh himself had experienced setbacks—being pushed out of a top job at Merrill Lynch following the global financial crisis in 1998 and then climbing back to become one of the most prominent executives on Wall Street. Ogilvie learned from people like Waugh that success takes time. "I've learned as much playing with these great businesspeople as they've learned from playing with me," Ogilvie told me.

I wondered what lessons Ogilvie might be willing to share. Several, it turned out. He offered what I've distilled down to nine essential lessons for creating and managing success.

1. Dream big, but plan wisely.

Ogilvie told me how when he was growing up in Ohio, he liked to read about business. His family watched *Moneyline* every night. "I always had a little business going on," he recalled. "As a kid, I mowed lawns. I invested some of the money I made and bought golf equipment with the rest." He knew he wanted to be a professional golfer when he decided to go to Duke. But he also saw Duke as an insurance policy just in case he couldn't make a living on his dream. By getting a good education, he not only gave himself a safety net but he gained the tools for running a business. As he found out when he came out on Tour, he'd need those financial skills to manage his golf career.

2. Tiger Woods and Warren Buffett have one thing in common.

Golf and business are very similar, almost parallel, Ogilvie told me. "In business, no two quarters are alike, no two days are alike, and no two challenges are alike," he said. "On the golf course you have wind, you have rain, you have slow greens and firm greens, greens that make balls spin back, greens that make the balls release.

Your environment is always changing. You have to know yourself really well. You have to know your strengths and your weaknesses and you have to come to grips with those and play to your strengths and play around your weaknesses." He explained that meant knowing when to be conservative and when to be aggressive. For him, right-hand pins were a challenge. At the beginning of his career he would go very aggressively at every pin. He had to learn to adjust. Now, he'll play to the middle of the green instead of trying to force in a shot that he normally didn't like. "When I look at Mr. Buffett and I look at Tiger Woods, the one similarity that they share together and that they are better at than anyone else in the world is discipline," he said. "I've spent time with Buffett—maybe we've had dinner five or six times and I've had Thanksgiving at his daughter's house. Talking to Buffett and seeing his discipline has helped my golf game a lot. He doesn't buy what he doesn't understand and he plays to his strengths. Phil Mickelson would be very close to Tiger Woods, and maybe even have a record, if he had that discipline. It's not that different than all the really smart people who got caught up in the dot-com deals."

3. Success is about the little things.

If you put Warren Buffett and Bill Gates and Tiger Woods in any situation they will do well. But between 31st and 101st on the money list (the difference between $2.1 million or $860,000 in 2006) it comes down to the intangibles of getting a shot or two better. In business it is also about the intangibles. It might start with where you went to business school. It helps to go to Harvard or Yale or Duke—not so much because of the education but because of the people around you. And then rising up has to do with where you start out. Do you start at Procter & Gamble or GE or do you start at a smaller, more entrepreneurial place? That can determine a lot about where a person's career goes. And then it comes down to how good you are at dealing with people, or how well you swallow your ego or control your emotions, or deal with a team. The corollary in golf is understanding where you excel. If you are a good bunker player, for example, you might not mind attempting a shot that will land on the beach if it isn't perfect.

4. Learn from failure.

"A lot of businesspeople have told me that you learn a lot more through adversity than triumph," he said. "For me, there are holes on tour where I have made big numbers and I now understand what I did wrong and what I have to do to get a ball in the fairway." Ogilvie said that when he makes a mistake and blows a round, he goes somewhere for an hour and beats himself up. Shortly after the Barclays, he had a chance to win at Chicago, shot 79 on Saturday, and fell from contention. At the end of the tournament, he dropped his wife and kids off at the airport so they could fly to New York. He then drove three hours to the next tournament. Along the way, he thought about what went wrong and where he went right. He realized that his regular routine on the course had disappeared. Under the pressure of being on the cusp of victory, he forgot everything and started playing his shots too quickly. "I didn't have a mechanism to step back and realize this was going on," he said. From that point on, he focused on managing his performance under pressure. The very next week he finished in the top 10. Three weeks later he shot his second 62 of the year to move into third place. "I did that by staying to my routine and not getting ahead of myself," he said.

5. You need to experience life to appreciate life.

After Duke, Ogilvie decided he wanted to see the world and play mini tours. He played in Asia, Europe, and South America. He had $8,000 from his family and had to play for his food. "I stripped the business down to the fundamentals," he said. "I lived at home when I wasn't on the mini tours. I drove a Nissan Sentra. We roomed two or three guys to a room. I did the basic things to get as cash-flow positive as I could." It wasn't easy. But he got to experience things that he'd never have experienced had he stayed in the United States. When he moved up to the Nationwide Tour and then the PGA Tour, he found that he could really appreciate what he now had and also what he'd seen.

6. You need to understand the capital markets.

Being a professional golfer is expensive. There is the cost of travel, fees to caddies, tournament entrance fees, and food. To cover costs, Ogilvie needed to raised $46,000 when he started on the Nationwide Tour. "I actually sold shares," he said. "The best players don't have to do this. But the majority of players do have some syndication." Ogilvie's syndicate of investors earned a 78 percent return in eight months. "The deal was that they got 80 percent of the first $46,000 I won on the golf course," he continued. "It was funny because they sent me the checks in mid-February and the following week I won a tournament and received a $45,000 check. So I wish I'd held off. Then out of the next $46,000, they got 50 percent and I kept 50 percent. And then the next $46,000 they got 10 percent and I got 90 percent. They were taking a risk because before they gave me the money, I missed my first three cuts."

7. Time management is key.

The toughest thing for any young player or rising business star is time management and learning how to say no. That means having a good agent and surrounding yourself with people you can trust. There are tremendous demands from charities and other commitments. You have to focus. "That is one way where golf and business are exactly the same," Ogilvie said.

8. Have a plan.

"When I first wanted to break 80, I broke out the golf course in three-hole intervals in which I could have two pars and a bogey," Ogilvie explained. "On a par-72, that got me to 78. Later on, depending on the course, I might set goals for six-hole intervals. As I get older, I look at how I can get better. I want ways to have 10 more years on tour and also be better in five years as well as in one month. I prepare for the 10-year financially. I prepare for the five-year physically, and the one-month mentally. I want 10 years more out here. Tour life is tough. I spend 270 nights a year away from home."

9. Don't worry about impressing those around you.

"In business and golf, when you are young you want the respect of your peers and you want people to see how good you are," Ogilvie said. "The bottom line is if you are good at what you do, people are going to notice you. I used to get nervous when I played with the top players. I'd want Phil Mickelson to think I was a good player. But Phil focuses on his game and as long as I'm out of his way and I'm fun to play with he won't care. He doesn't care if I shoot 64. That was tough to get used to. At the end of the day, the guys don't really care how good you are."

Golf is about patience

Insurance executive Jerry Jurgensen is a legendary CEO in professional golf circles. When his company, Nationwide, swooped in to pick up the sponsorship of a struggling developmental tour, a lot of people thought he was crazy. Jurgensen has been proven right by the success of the Nationwide Tour and its impact on his bottom line. Along with making savvy business decisions, Jurgensen is an avid player who ranks among the top two CEO golfers in the *Fortune* 500.

"The same success factors apply to business [as to golf]. You need self-confidence, patience, and perseverance. Guys in their late thirties are still clawing and scratching to make it, and they are as good as anyone I've ever seen. The hardest thing about the PGA Tour is getting on the PGA Tour. People have a notion that it's a glamorous life, but it's a grind. You drive everywhere because you can't afford to fly. A few years ago, [Mark] Hensby was living in his car. In 2003 the Nationwide Tour champion, Chris Couch, was down to his last $100 when one of his buddies loaned him $500 for the entry fee and food for one more event, and he won it. These players have wonderful messages to convey to the youth of America about hard work."

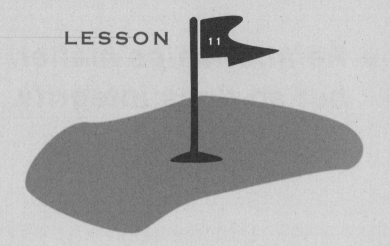

LESSON 11

Relationships matter, but so does integrity.

The CEO Woodstock

IT WAS FEBRUARY at the Pebble Beach Golf Links, time for the annual CEO showdown known as the AT&T Pebble Beach Pro-Am. Amid the crashing waves of the Pacific and bellowing sea lions, dozens of America's most powerful business leaders were spread out across the lush fairways. I was accompanying one of the foursomes, walking inside the ropes and talking golf and business with my host.

The format of the event teams one amateur with one professional. Most television viewers tune in to watch Bill Murray and Ray Romano joke around with the galleries or to see normally intense players like Vijay Singh in a more relaxed setting. The real action, however, is what you don't get to see on TV. Dotting the fairways was a who's who of corporate power. Many began arriving two days earlier, landing one G4 after another until the tiny

Monterey County Airport looked like a showroom for corporate jets. The three courses that host the tournament—Pebble Beach, Spyglass, and Poppy Hills—were a living, breathing edition of the *Fortune* 500 dotted with real estate tycoons, investment bankers, and media chieftains.

Among the powerful was H. Wayne Huizenga, the founder of Blockbuster, Waste Management, and Auto Nation. Mr. H, as he is known to his employees, had flown in following a practice session at his personal golf course in Florida. Not to be outdone, Donald Trump arrived with the latest plans for another championship course of his own. Other attendees might not have owned golf courses but had still greater influence. Teddy Forstmann has pulled off some of the biggest deals in corporate history. Venture capitalist Don Valentine has provided the startup capital for Cisco Systems. Investor Bill Gross is recognized as the most important figure in financial markets next to the Fed chairman. Brokerage chief Charles Schwab revolutionized the stock market. Merrill Lynch's Stan O'Neal rebuilt his fading company into the bull of Wall Street. Media magnate Les Moonves of Viacom was at the top of the corporate game. The tournament's unofficial host, Pebble Beach owner, Peter Ueberroth, personally selected many of the attendees.

So great was the concentration of power and wealth that one *Fortune* 500 CEO in attendance quickly dubbed the gathering "the CEO Woodstock." Only instead of bongs and the Grateful Dead, it was birdies and Bing Crosby (who started the tournament as his annual clambake). Investment bankers could be overheard trading golf tips with CEOs at dinner parties thrown by Forstmann at the elite Club XIX, by Charles Schwab at the stately Beach Club, and in the private homes of others. Mutual fund managers commiserated with rivals at hedge funds about putts thwarted by the mythical cellophane bridge over the hole. Others recalled the time

Australian media mogul Kerry Packer won the event, reportedly with an inflated handicap. You could even hear gossip about a certain pro golfer, a former number one in the world, who inelegantly told the sponsor of another tourament that he'd only play if he was provided with a female escort.

It was a fun, almost raucous time—sort of like returning to the fraternity house 20 years after college. There were even groupies. You probably never imagined that young girls would want to throw themselves at 65-year-old venture capitalists. Of course, most of the women were after the touring pros. In the evenings by the putting green, they'd cluster around the players and make overtures. What was all the more shocking was that some of the most powerful businesspeople in the world looked like giddy sidekicks as their professional playing partners snuck off with women they had just met.

And there I was right in the thick of it. I was marching along the fairways, inside the ropes, along with a group of wives that was watching their husbands play in the tournament. Among the women was Susan, the stunning wife of Tour player Andrew Magee, an amiable, intelligent man whom I'd met for drinks the night before at the home of a prominent executive. Unlike many of the wives you meet on the Tour, she wasn't a blond. Nor was she trying to be. She was the sort of woman that the other CEO wives could hang out with because she was funny and also a bit wiser than most of the Tour wives. She acted like a chaperone of sorts. At one point, she got into a heated conversation with the frosty-haired girlfriend of a married top pro. The girlfriend complained that she wasn't getting the respect she deserved from the pro golfer wives. "I pick out his shirts and pants," the woman shouted. "I'm his *Tour* wife." To which Susan shouted back, "Maybe you should ask his other wife about that—the one who's home taking care of his three kids."

Susan knew the golf business, from the agents to the club-makers. She knew which players had lost money in the stock market and which ones had the best relationships with CEOs. I told her how great I thought it was that all these CEOs were friends. She turned and looked at me as if I were a fool. "You know," she said, "everything here is about business."

And she was right. Everywhere you looked business was happening. Not so much in direct ways but in a thousand subtle ways that fall into place whenever the movers and shakers step onto the first tee. Even if no one ever mentioned a specific deal, they were implicit because at this lofty level deals result from relationships—and at Pebble Beach, many of the men had been friends for years. They had served together on corporate boards, on presidential commissions, and on the Business Roundtable, a powerful forum for CEOs. They'd invested in the same hedge funds and hired one another's children for summer jobs. They even played golf wearing similar white turtlenecks and khakis. What's more, they sponsored each other for membership in the best clubs. You could see the badges of these interlocking relationships emblazoned on jackets, ties, and belt buckles—the lone cypress of Cypress Point in California, the striped shield of Pine Valley in New Jersey, the Indian Chief of Seminole in Florida, the red flag of Augusta National in Georgia, and the understated emblems of a dozen or so other preeminent private clubs.

My point is that business in this world is not overt. It's more like a secret handshake. What the average salesman or aspiring executive doesn't understand is that only rarely do transactions occur in this setting. That's not to suggest that business isn't being conducted on the course or that these relationships don't frequently morph into deals. Why else do members of Cypress Point often bring top clients to play? Members of the National Golf Links—overwhelmingly comprising top CEOs like Ken Chennault of American Express—make it a habit to send their top salespeople out for the day with clients. The foursomes feast on lobster before the round and drinks around the fireplace after, and business is very clearly the objective. During one such round, I overheard one of my playing partners tell another, "We'll be sure to do more business with you next quarter."

Dealmaking is at the core. At Augusta, it is rumored that one member, a local stockbroker, has a thick book of business thanks to his contacts at the club. Jack Welch put Scott McNealy onto GE's board of directors after they became golf buddies. Welch, in fact, made golf seem like a prerequisite for corporate success during his 20-year tenure. While looking for a successor at GE, he hosted candidates at Augusta to see how they handled themselves. He ultimately settled on Jeff Immelt, who was vacationing at his home on golf mecca Kiawah Island when he got the big call.

But for the most part, these and other stories formed around the notion of a relationship. The idea here is that you can never learn as much about a person in his office as you will on the course. The reason is that golf is a litmus test for character and trustworthiness. On one occasion, for example, the famed executive recruiter Gerry Roche was caught on the course during a lightning storm. He ran for shelter and found himself on a bench next to a man who turned out to be the then-CEO of RJR Nabisco, Lou Gerstner. The two had never met. But Gerstner's incredibly direct and intense style caught Roche's attention. Some time later, he recruited Gerstner to be CEO of IBM, a role that cemented Gerstner's reputation as a turnaround artist. Interestingly, however, what one person sees as a positive character trait another can see as a flaw. After taking the helm at IBM in 1997, Gerstner was profiled by *Fortune* writer Betsy Morris. The article portrayed Gerstner as the same hard-nosed boss who first caught the attention of Roche and the IBM board. Morris recounted a scene at the Medalist Golf Club in Hobe Sound, Florida, during which the hurried Gerstner boorishly played through a foursome he believed was moving too slowly. Despite the fact that almost everyone in the business world knew this was exactly how Gerstner behaved, the IBM CEO became incensed by the description. He pulled all IBM advertising from the magazine and forbid company executives from interacting with *Fortune* for years. Though few would admit this publicly, the very character traits that convinced IBM to hire him were seen by other top CEOs as evidence that Gerstner was arrogant.

Which gets us to the reason why golf is such a character test. It is not so much the skill of a player as it is the behavior of a player. I suppose there is something to be learned from whether a player has the guts to go for it in 2 on a par-5 or whether a player knocks a ball laterally from the woods or plays the low percentage shot. The greater insight comes from their actual behavior. Former Banc One CEO John McCoy once told me about the time he was playing Muirfield Village with a prospective senior executive. After hitting a shot poorly, the man heaved his club into a pond. He didn't get the job. In a similar display of poor behavior, the investor Ken Langone, one of the founders of Home Depot, recalls playing in a club tournament in California when he noticed that his partner's ball had moved. Not a slight rotation, but a good old-fashioned "foot wedge" to the left out of an ugly lie. "I couldn't believe it," Langone recalled. "He had no honor. This was a tournament. We were partners, so it didn't hurt me. But he acted with total disregard for the rules of the game. I decided right at that moment that there was no way I was going to let us win." He paused, then added, "And there was no way I would ever do business with his company again."

I can recall my own similar story. I had a friend named Joe. We worked together and played golf whenever we had free time.

I admired Joe as a colleague. He was older than me and knew more about the world. He treated me like a younger brother. Then one day we were having a match. I was teamed with another colleague named John. Joe was teamed with Jed. My team was one up through 15 holes when I sprayed my tee shot into the woods on the par-4 sixteenth hole. My ball was barely visible from the pine needles but I played it out sideways—a costly penalty—and ended the hole with a double-bogey. John also recorded a 6 and we lost the hole by a stroke. On the seventeenth, an almost identical hole, Joe sliced his ball into the woods while I split the fairway with my best tee shot of the day. Joe approached his ball, lifted it, and tossed it into the fairway. I asked him if he was taking a penalty. "Are you kidding?" he answered. He grabbed a fairway wood and flew his ball onto the green from where he 2-putted for par to tie me. We tied again on 18. Sitting in the bar afterward, Joe tallied up the scores and then announced, "You guys owe us $5 each." I was flabbergasted. I told Joe that he needed to count a penalty for his wayward tee shot. He insisted that he did nothing wrong. Hoping to cool things down, John gave Joe and Jed two $5 bills. I simmered visibly. Because we were in a job that depended on people trusting the facts we reported, I wondered whether I could ever trust Joe again. Then several years later, now at another job, a colleague told me Joe had applied for a position. I was asked to provide a character reference. I declined and Joe didn't get the job.

So what does all this teach us? From my experience at Pebble Beach, I can say that relationships are justifiably important in business. We need to be able to trust our partners. But sometimes we let relationships get in our way or convince ourselves that the same playing partner who is smiling at us on the course won't turn around and stab us in the back over a business deal. One of the people playing in the AT&T was the CEO of a major investment firm who was widely known among fellow CEOs for his charm but also for his aloofness toward employees. When one of his Wall Street counterparts asked him for a recommendation letter to join a prestigious private club, the CEO gladly agreed to offer an endorsement. He even sent a copy of the letter to the other CEO. Then privately he contacted the membership committee and told them to disregard his letter. This caused an uproar at the club and almost led to the CEO being expelled. To this day, he refuses to admit that any of this happened. I once asked another CEO why he liked doing business with this CEO. "It's about relationships," he said. "We've played together for years and I trust him."

Then I told him about the incident and the CEO gave me a rather shocked look and asked, "He did what?"

LESSON 12

Don't fear taking risks.

The Greatest Land Deal

IT WAS A SCORCHING DAY at the golf course. Pat McKinney and Leonard Long, two business partners, were standing on the practice putting green of the Cassique course at the Kiawah Island Club in South Carolina waiting for their other partner, Buddy Darby. Darby was the senior partner in the relationship and, as was his custom, he was late for his tee time. When he finally arrived, he walked briskly to the practice green and greeted his partners with a powerful handshake. A broad-shouldered man with the flair of a former quarterback, he turned to a caddy who was waiting with his golf clubs, reached for a driver, and promptly teed up two balls side by side on the velvety putting surface. "Gimme a second," he said before taking two huge swings and sending the balls flying out in the direction of the driving range. He then turned to McKinney and Long and declared, "Okay. I'm ready."

Kiawah Island is famous for its golf. Located a short distance from Charleston, the barrier island came to international prominence as the host site of the 1991 Ryder Cup, known to golf fans as the "war by the shore" because of the rowdy partisanship between the American and European teams and the gallery. But to me, Kiawah is also a story about one of the smartest real estate transactions since Peter Minuet bought the island of Manhattan in 1689—smarter even than the purchase of Pebble Beach in 1999. What makes the story all the more remarkable is that the purchase of Kiawah was made by three men, then in their thirties, who had to go against the grain of popular consensus to pull it off—and in the process, narrowly dodged failure on multiple occasions.

In the interests of disclosure, I've vacationed on Kiawah for the past decade and I'm a member of the private club on the island. During that time, I've gotten to know the island's developers and their story. The first of the three partners I met was McKinney. McKinney is the salesman. He runs the real estate operation. He grew up in a modest household in Atlanta and put himself through college as a door-to-door Bible salesman. After school, two fellow Bible salesmen convinced him to become a real estate salesman at Sea Pines in Hilton Head in 1971. He became director of real estate sales a year later. Then in 1975, he moved to Charleston to take over Kiawah's fledgling sales operation. The one demand he made before accepting the job was that the Kuwaiti development company, which owned the island, change its plans for golf on Kiawah. At the time, plans called for building an "executive" course for time-constrained conventioneers. McKinney insisted that the island have a regulation-length golf course. When he arrived, there were only a handful of ramshackle homes built near the ocean, an old plantation house that belonged to its original owners, and the footings of a resort hotel that would soon open. He spent four years building the sales team—increasing sales from nothing to $60 million—but then quit to become a minority partner in a nearby development called Wild Dunes, which was controlled by Buddy Darby's family. He worked there until 1984 when he set off to run his own development company.

Darby himself is from a prominent Charleston family. His grandfather, J. C. Long, had purchased the Isle of Palms just north of Charleston at the end of World War II and turned it into one of the first modern-day seaside communities. Darby was a risk taker. He had played high school and college football and liked to throw himself into difficult situations.

Leonard Long is Buddy's cousin and happened to be one of the best real estate lawyers in South Carolina.

The story of how these three men came together to buy the island began in 1675, when the British crown acquired the 2,700-acre island off the coast of South Carolina for cloth, trinkets, and beads from the Kiawah Indians. Then in 1699, a suspected pirate and associate of the legendary Captain Kidd named George Raynor was given control of the island. Raynor's heirs eventually sold the land to John Stanyarne, an affluent planter, who used Kiawah for cattle ranching and growing indigo. Upon his death in 1772, the island was split between Stanyarne's granddaughters, Mary Gibbes and Elizabeth Vanderhorst. During the Revolutionary War, sick and wounded officers were sent to Kiawah for rest and recreation, but little else happened on the island. It was simply one of the countless barrier islands where few sane people wanted to live. One letter written during the mid-1850s compared Kiawah to Botany Bay, the Australian penal colony that was considered unlivable, and described victims of assorted snake bites and illnesses caught while attempting to plant crops that were routinely destroyed by natural disasters. In 1951, ownership passed hands to a lumberman named C. C. Royal, who paid $123,000 and probably expected to clear-cut the entire place.

Then, in 1974, Royal's heirs sold the same land to a Kuwaiti-backed resort developer for $18.2 million.

During their first decade on the island, the Kuwaitis prospered. They opened two golf courses and a hotel. But by the mid-1980s the Kuwaitis were no longer happy with the island. Sales had plunged to $13 million. Rumors began circulating around Charleston that they wanted out. Companies like Equitable and MetLife had reportedly inquired about buying Kiawah. But all had been rebuffed by a young Kuwaiti named Sal Alzouman, who was in charge of the island's development. Then, soon after the stock market collapse of 1987, McKinney and his business partner received a tip from a Kiawah sales agent. The Kuwaiti minister of finance had shown up unannounced and demanded a tour of the island. The minister was enraged by the slow pace of development he saw. Later, behind closed doors, he and Alzouman had gotten into a shouting match, which sales agents listened to with their ears practically pressed to the door. Alzouman suddenly emerged, red faced, and announced, "I've just been ordered to sell the damn island."

McKinney swung into action. He sensed that something big could come out of Kiawah. And the rumored price was right. Years earlier, the Kuwaitis had privately discussed selling the island for $600 million. Now McKinney thought he might pull it off for under $150 million. The catch was that Alzouman wouldn't take his phone calls. He needed a front man. But as obvious as the deal seemed to him, there were few takers. He went through three or four variations of partnerships—and even secured an option to buy the island based on his ability to raise additional funding. And each fell apart. It was at this point that fate came into play. While McKinney was making the rounds trying to get backing, Darby and Long had hatched their own plan to make a run for the island. It began one afternoon when the *Charleston Evening Post* arrived on Buddy's doorstep. The edition featured an article stating that the group McKinney had cobbled together behind a prominent local broadcasting executive had given up its option to purchase the island. Darby had spent minimal time on Kiawah but the idea of buying an undeveloped island with 14 miles of beachfront property and endless salt marshes surrounding premier golf courses seemed like a no-brainer. There's some debate over who actually hatched the idea but Buddy and Leonard lobbied the family for the financial and political support they needed to pull off a deal. At the time, the family business was run by a distinguished gentleman named Charlie Way, Buddy's uncle and Leonard's cousin. Getting Way's support was essential because he had the gravitas that they lacked. Then they got in touch with McKinney and his partners. The story goes that in March 1988, Charlie Way walked into Alzouman's office, introduced himself, and declared that he was going to buy Kiawah. He placed a $1 million cashier's check on the desk as a nonrefundable deposit. Alzouman said he'd think about it but Way insisted, "We're either going to buy Kiawah today or forget it."

Way and Alzouman spent the night negotiating the terms while Buddy, Leonard, and Pat hung out in an eight-passenger Suburban and ran over the terms during the few breaks when Way was able to emerge from the meeting. At 2 A.M., Alzouman turned to Way and declared, "Congratulations, now it's your fucking island."

The price was $105 million. The partners had just a few weeks to secure financing and began crisscrossing the country in search of backers. They contacted 15 of the most prominent institutional investors in the country—General Electric Capital and Equitable among them—and offered to give away 50 percent of the deal in exchange for financing. They were flatly rejected by all until a local investor stepped in. Over the following years, the partners would pay back the debt, cede control from the local family, and become millionaires many times over.

Things seemed to be going incredibly well. A couple years after the deal, Kiawah was slated to host the Ryder Cup, the semi-annual match between the United States and Europe. Real estate sales were setting records. The only concern the three young partners had was that a real estate crisis would hit the country or some sort of environmental calamity like a major hurricane would hit Charleston. Kiawah could survive either. As luck would have it, the partners found themselves confronted with both potential disasters. Hurricane Hugo deluged and tore up Charleston in the fall of 1989. This was while crews were still building the Ocean Course, which would host the Ryder Cup. Buddy was in Europe at the time watching the European team tie the Americans at The Belfry when he heard the news that the Ocean Course had practically vanished. He flew back to Charleston. It was impossible to reach Kiawah by car, so he rented a helicopter and flew out to the island. From the sky above the Ocean Course site, he looked down and saw architect Pete Dye riding a tractor. Dye was trying to save whatever he could of the course—and probably make a few changes that wouldn't have gotten through the environmental regulators had there not been a destructive storm.

If that wasn't bad enough, then came the second event—and this one was even more of a threat. By the early 1990s, the real estate market had collapsed under the weight of the savings and loan scandal. Darby had sold off Kiawah's resort assets to the Landmark hotel company to offset some costs of the deal. But Landmark was heavily involved in the S&L situation and filed for bankruptcy soon after the Ryder Cup. Though the assets were acquired—at a bargain price at auction—by another investor, the greater concern for Darby, Long, and McKinney was what would happen to the value of their holdings. It was at this point that the three partners began to mold themselves into a team that utilized the strengths of each member to reach a common goal. Darby was always the most confident of the three. He was great with big-picture stuff like coming up with the concept for a private club on the island, which eventually included two golf courses, a beach club, and a spa. Long was great with details. He could oversee the projects and make sure things like antiques and hand-carved railings were perfect. He could spend hours poring over art samples and then engage in a heated debate of environmental laws that could be used to protect the group's investment. McKinney could then take the vision and the details and sell the idea to future residents who would pay increasingly large sums of money to make Kiawah their home. At times they must have hated each other. For certain, egos got involved. But the three never forgot the singular idea that Kiawah was not so much an investment as a legacy. It worked because over the last 20 years, the three have sold more than $1 billion or so in land and maintained a pristine environment on Kiawah that is unmatched among the barrier islands.

And so I found myself on that scorching day wondering what I might learn from these three men. Over 18 holes, I could see their personalities perfectly defined. Darby was either far down the fairway or deep in the woods. Long seemed more interested in talking than playing. And McKinney was an accurate, feisty competitor who didn't give in even when the odds didn't look good. They seemed so different. And yet they were clearly partners who listened to each other. They'd come through a lot together. Looking back, it seems like an easy decision—several thousand acres for sales at pennies on the dollar. But that is today. They could have easily lost it all. I asked Darby why he was willing to risk it. His response spoke for all three: "Sometimes, you have to take a chance."

Golf is about being bold

Known to his employees as Mr. H, Harry Wayne Huizenga, owner of the Miami Dolphins, loves to create companies. Among his credits are Waste Management, Blockbuster, and AutoNation. He likes the game of golf so much that he built his own course.

"It's called the Floridian. Gary Player designed it. About 150 friends and business associates of mine play there and nobody pays fees or dues. We have lots of fun. For a few years we held an event, the Big Three Invitational, with Arnie Palmer, Jack Nicklaus, and Gary, and we still host a fund-raiser for the Gary Player Foundation. Ray Floyd likes to play the Floridian; so do Chi Chi Rodriguez, Nick Price, Greg Norman, and Jesper Parnevik.

"I play a lot with Dan Marino. We've been to Ireland together. Dan is unbelievably competitive. I'm a 12-handicap and he's about a 4, so he gives me strokes. We always bet. The amount doesn't matter; we just have to have a bet going."

Are businessmen as hard-nosed on the course as quarterbacks?

"Jack Welch is. Jack brings out the best in me. Before his back surgery he was a 6-handicap, just as focused and competitive a golfer as Dan."

LESSON 13

Be nice to your caddy.

Loopers Who Made It Big

I **WAS PLAYING** the National Golf Links on Long Island with a
few friends. We had this very effective caddy who happened to
be a Shinnecock Indian. He and I got to talking and I asked
him how the members, who include a number of so-called titans
of business, treat the caddies.

"Some are okay, sir, but a lot aren't that nice," he said. "A lot
of them blame us if they hit a bad shot or they miss a putt."

I don't think he was complaining, because I've seen quite a
few guys beat up on their caddies for what they think are misread
putts or poor club selections. Never mind that it's the golfer who
has to execute. Other than the fact that this behavior will make
your playing partners think you're a real jerk, acting this way could
backfire years after you walk off the eighteenth green. What I'm
getting at is that some of the most successful businesspeople I
know started out as caddies. Jack Welch was a caddy at a club in

Boston when he was 12. The game caught his attention and he spent his time as a looper studying the swings of better players. He incorporated their techniques into his own swing and became an accomplished player. This certainly helped him develop relationships as a young General Electric executive. Bill Gross, who as chief investment officer of Pimco is arguably the second most powerful person in financial markets, started caddying at Los Altos Country Club in Los Altos, California, when he was a young boy. Chris Sullivan, the co-founder of Outback Steakhouse, started caddying for his father when he was seven years old. He was a player by the time he turned 11 and became so enamored with the game that during college he worked part time as a bartender so to earn enough money to cover his golf fees. The bartending gig turned into a restaurant career that led to founding Outback.

Indeed, some fairly prominent executives have used their caddy experiences to catapult themselves to success. One of my favorite caddy stories involves Peter Ueberroth. Ueberroth made his name running the 1984 Olympics and later becoming commissioner of Major League Baseball. Ueberroth grew up in the Chicago area in the 1950s. His family didn't have much money. So to make ends meet, Ueberroth became a caddy at Sunset Ridge Country Club in Northfield, Illinois. "I owe a lot to the caddiemaster because he had us double-bagging, one bag on each shoulder," Ueberroth told me in an interview for *T&L Golf*. "That really built me up and made me strong enough to play football and baseball. Ultimately it helped me get a water polo scholarship, which was my only way of going to college."

Ueberroth, who still wasn't much of a golfer, chose San Jose State. As part of his training, he'd spend hours running along the beach. One such beach happened to be adjacent to the Pebble Beach Golf Links. Ueberroth would climb the cliffs and watch golfers hitting across the eighth and ninth holes. He fell in love with the game. A few decades later, he put together the investment group that purchased and now operates Pebble Beach.

Then there's famed investor Peter Lynch. Lynch grew up in Boston, where his father was a math professor at Boston College. When the elder Lynch died of cancer, 11-year-old Peter volunteered to become a caddy at a nearby course to make money. As he carried clubs up and down the fairways, he'd overhear golfers talk about investments. Though the Lynch family seemed ideologically opposed to the stock market, the younger Lynch became fascinated with stocks. He caddied throughout high school and then won a scholarship named after the legendary amateur golfer Frances Ouimet, who had also caddied to make extra money and later won the U.S. Open in 1913. While caddying, Lynch got to know a man named George Sullivan, who happened to be the president of Fidelity. Sullivan encouraged Lynch to apply for a summer job with the company. Lynch got the job and went on to make history as one of the greatest stock investors of all time.

Proving that life moves in circles, I'm reminded of another great story that happened thanks to Ouiment. Eddie Lowery was just 10 years old when he caddied for Ouimet during his triumphant U.S. Open. Years later, Lowery moved to California and became a multimillionaire auto dealer. He used his financial success to support the careers of promising amateur golfers such as Ken Venturi, who himself won the U.S. Open in 1964.

LESSON 14

Learn to manage expectations.

How to *Think* the Game

I FIRST MET JOHN HOBBINS when I was struggling with an incurable fade. After years of playing, I'd somehow practiced my way into a swing that produced a shot that slid weakly to the right. This was more than just a swing issue because it was making it more difficult for me to play with colleagues, clients, and sources. I wasn't having fun and it showed. John not only fixed my flaw, but also taught me a new appreciation for the game. John is the most passionate student of the golf swing I've ever met. He runs the Greenside Golf Academy in New York. Because he's located in the corporate capital of the world, his students are almost all Wall Street executives, prominent venture capitalists, and powerful politicians. Many of these people hire John to run corporate events for their companies, and as a result, he has a unique perspective on golf and business.

What have you learned about business and golf from your students?

What I see most of when it comes to business and golf is that although these people are very successful in business, they don't normally assess their golf games the same way they assess their businesses. Managing your golf like your business is rather common sense to me. My recommendation is that they look at their strengths, weaknesses, what they are good at, and where they need to improve. When it comes to their golf game, there is never an assessment done of whether they are a better short-game player or a better putter or chipper or driver of the ball. And they do not play within themselves. I can't tell you the number of times I'll see a student on the course who has 225 yards to the green. He knows he can't reach it. But instead of hitting a shot 125 yards or 150 yards, he'll go for it and take double bogey.

Just as you evaluate your company and determine what your company is capable of achieving, you should evaluate your golf game. Instead, I see guys who manage risk all day take a gambling approach on the golf course that almost guarantees they will never shoot as low a score as they are capable of shooting.

What makes you think these players aren't the same in their professional lives?

I talk to them about their businesses and I know how they act in the workplace and how they think of their businesses. I was a psychology major in college, and I want to know how people think.

So is the issue that people who are successful in business can't understand why they're not as successful in golf?

No. It's a matter of having no assessment. If your company is making an acquisition, the first thing you do is look at the target company's financials, then its strengths and weaknesses and figure out a plan. You've got to do the same thing to be a better golfer. Let's say you hit your 5 iron and 6 iron better than any other clubs. Then you want to put yourself into position to have those clubs in your hands. You are managing to your skills.

Where do you see the most common weaknesses?

I see them in course management. A wonderful example happened with a CEO during a playing lesson one day. I was paying more attention to his game than mine and on a par-5 I hit my drive into a cluster of trees off the right side of the fairway. I had no shot but to hit it out sideways with a 5 iron and could not advance it forward. When I was preparing to play the shot out sideways the CEO asked what I was doing. I explained that I had played a poor drive and I was playing back to the fairway rather than attempting to hit it up through the trees to advance it forward. The CEO said that since the trees were 90 percent air, why not try it? I explained to him that screen doors were also 90 percent air but I would not play through them either. I proceeded to play my third shot down the fairway to about 75 yards short of the green, where I hit a sand wedge to 12 feet and made the putt for par. The CEO then stated that I was fortunate to have made par and insinuated that I was lucky. I agreed on both accounts but also pointed out to him that I created my own luck through thoughtful planning and execution. The worst score I was going to make with my plan was bogey and I had salvaged par. The moral of the story, if you will, is to accept that when you play golf you will always hit a bad shot. It is not usually that shot that hurts you in scoring but your reaction to that shot and then the subsequent shots that you play as a result. Had this been a business transaction the CEO would not have played the shot through the trees, as it offered very little chance for success and the risk/reward was not worth it.

So through course management, I can lower my score without actually striking the ball better?

Yes. Sometimes a bogey is as good as a par. Play to ensure you get bogey and then every now and then you'll sink a putt for par. But avoid the big number.

How can people possibly manage their game when they are playing with other people and talking business?

It's a cliché but they have to play one shot at a time. This is not something that comes easily. It starts with managing emotions and treating a birdie like a bogey and then thinking at the start of each shot where the smartest place is to end up so that you can get the lowest possible score. It's a matter of playing to your strengths.

Golf is about knowing
what's around you

Onetime bartender and waiter Chris Sullivan co-founded Outback Steakhouse in 1987. He remains chairman of the company but squeezes in enough time to work on his golf game. In fact, he managed to merge golf and business by making his company's Bloomin' Onion blimp a frequent site in the skies above many PGA events.

"Back in 1987, my partner Bob Basham and I had sold a Chili's joint venture and were looking to create a new business. The craze around the country was for health food, but there were still long lines outside quality steakhouses. So we recruited an old buddy of mine from New Orleans to run the food side of the business and opened our first restaurant in Tampa, where I live.

"I started caddying for my dad when I was seven. He was in the FBI and he'd play with his buddies on Saturdays. He started having me hit golf balls in the backyard, and then I started playing on courses when I was about eleven. In college, I worked as a waiter and a bartender. I liked working at night because I could play golf during the day. Ever since then I've played two or three times a week.

"[Golf has taught me] that I'm going to make mistakes, but every hole I get to start over fresh. I use that in

continued

business, too. You can't get bogged down. You have to treat every day as a fresh start. Golf has taught me how to act under pressure, and that if I lighten up a little on golf—and in regular life—it is a much better experience."

LESSON 15

Be a generous teacher.

The Pro

MICHAEL CHERNACK DRESSES in a white shirt almost every day, along with striped tie and neatly pressed slacks. Each morning he arrives at the Allianz Global Investors office in Stamford, Connecticut, and sits behind a trading-style desk surrounded by other identical desks. His is strewn with financial reports, calling lists, and memos. Within reach is a book penned by the famed investor Ben Graham, a dictionary of finance, and an autographed copy of a book written by Arnold Palmer. At one side of the desk is a hickory-shafted "mashie" from the 1920s, and on the wall is a photo from a favorite foursome that played Shinnecock next to a letter written from billionaire financier Ken Langone.

It could be the desk of any broker or salesman. But in this case it is the desk of a man who has made the unusual step of giving up his life as a PGA professional at one of America's most prestigious private clubs to become a Wall Street cub. As Chernack put it, "I learned the meaning of success from some of the most powerful people in business."

Chernack, 39, has certainly come far. Born in Queens, New York, he grew up on Long Island in a middle-class household. His parents were high school sweethearts who married when they were just 18. His dad worked as a carpenter—and became an estimator after losing an eye during a workplace accident—while his mother looked after Mike and his siblings. No one in the family played golf—including Mike, who played rugby. With the exception of one or two visits to a driving range with buddies, Mike never touched a club until he was in his twenties.

What changed his life was the day a golf catalog arrived at home. Mike had always loved equipment—sparkling-new hockey sticks, the fresh leather smell of a new baseball glove, an unblemished football—but golf was much more. There were so many parts and gadgets. Shortly after seeing the catalog, he walked into a golf store that was about to open and asked for a job. Now, it never occurred to me that anyone could go from retail salesman to general manager of a prestigious private club. I might have reconsidered quitting the college job I had selling clubs had I known that. But that's just what happened to Mike. He was a student at St. John's University in Queens at the time but practically stopped going to classes because he loved being around the equipment so much.

He excelled at the job. He learned the business of golf under the tutelage of an old club pro who had lost his job after having an affair with the club president's wife and was now working at the store. The old pro taught him how to sell and taught him how to listen to people. Mike didn't need to learn to love the game; that came naturally. The two would venture out to the golf course when they weren't working, and Mike learned the game from playing as a guest on a variety of private and public courses, often teeing it up at a track named Douglaston where players were a mix of off-duty cops, firefighters, construction workers, and the occasional lawyer or small-business owner who had snuck out for the afternoon. On weekends, he and a group of other players would set up teams for money games. The first time Mike played 18 holes he broke 100. Six months later he was shooting in the mid-80s. He wasn't Tiger Woods, but he had a natural way on the course.

In 1993, Mike took a job as the third assistant professional at a private club in North Hempstead, Long Island. Third assistant means you are pretty much starting at the lowest step on the ladder. He carried bags, washed down clubs, and ran the golf shop. He earned his membership as a teacher in the PGA of America, and he loved every minute of his job. While other assistant pros really just wanted to focus on their own games, Chernack had concluded early on that he was never going to make it on the PGA Tour. What he loved was running the pro shop and teaching. He was a fast success. And then a few years later, around 2001, he got the chance to work at one of the great private clubs in the country.

Deepdale, located in Manhasset, opened in 1955 and is considered one of architect Dick Wilson's best courses. It has gently rolling terrain, sharp doglegs, and slippery greens. You could spend all day on the fairways and never find a weed. The club handles a mere 4,000 rounds per year and is often empty (about three foursomes a day). What's remarkable about Deepdale, however, is not the condition of the course or the availability of tee times but the names in the locker room. The roster of members includes financiers such as Pete Peterson, Teddy Forstmann, Herb Allen, Richard Rainwater, Ken Langone, Ace Greenberg, Eric Gleacher. More than a dozen of the members are billionaires.

Many also belong to Augusta National, Shinnecock, and Cypress Point. To be clear, these are some of the greatest dealmakers in the world and Deepdale is often their private conference room.

It was not a grandiose entrance for Chernack. He took a pay cut and went back to being an assistant professional. Soon, however, he became known among the membership for his teaching talents and his good nature. He always greeted people with a broad smile and showed a genuine interest in helping them improve their play. "These were captains of industry, guys whose names were in the *Wall Street Journal* and who were billionaires," Chernack says. "But what I saw were people who loved the game, loved to practice, and understood that the game takes effort."

Mike taught the members about golf and they taught him about success. He noticed how they paid attention to detail—and respected others who did the same. Many were almost hypersensitive to their surroundings. No one wanted to talk business on the course but they were interested in hearing other people's opinions about political, social, and economic issues. He learned to tell the difference between members who wanted to be treated like royalty and members who wanted to forget how powerful they really were and just shoot the breeze with caddies. Giving lessons showed him what made people nervous or feel awkward. He learned how to be critical without seeming harsh. Most of all, he learned the importance of being authentic. "People like this can spot a phony from a mile away," he says. "I learned that 'please' and 'thank you' can take you very far in life if they come from you with genuine feeling."

Getting to know the members made Mike wonder if he could succeed in their world. He had serious doubts because he hadn't gone to an Ivy League school or been raised or trained in the best investment houses. His wife, Michelle, worked for a respected

investment bank named Sandler O'Neill. Sandler, which had trag-
ically lost a huge percentage of its employees in the World Trade
Center attack on September 11, 2001, was run by Deepdale member Jimmy Dunne. Though Mike had never really thought he was
capable to doing anything outside of golf, being around Dunne
taught him that taking risks was part of life. "I realized that a lot of
things I had always held close to me could help me in business, that
I could start from scratch—the little things that I pay attention to
are much more valuable than slick sales techniques."

Mike sought out a half dozen of his favorite members and
asked if they thought he had what it took to make it on Wall
Street. He never hit them up directly for jobs. He simply asked
for candid advice. They were more than encouraging. Several
worked with him to focus his goals and determine where he would
be able to make the quickest impact. One put him in touch with
a firm that eventually offered him a job.

Mike was hired as a junior executive, and found himself bearing the brunt of abusive bosses. He quickly discovered that the
only reason he had been given the job was so that the firm could
milk his Deepdale connections. This probably sounds like he was
naïve at the start—and he would agree. But the worst part was
that he was stuck. He didn't know where to turn. He certainly
couldn't go back to his golf friends because they'd assume he
wasn't cut out for Wall Street.

Then one day he heard from his wife that a prominent investment fund was having a special celebration at its headquarters in
Boston. One of the principals in the business was young Deepdale member named Bart O'Connor. O'Connor had been something of a mentor for Chernack, so Chernack called O'Connor
and asked to be invited. Since he didn't have any business cards,
Chernack printed up personal cards showing that he was a PGA

member. The celebration was no little event. Some of the most influential names in finance would be there. "I remember getting nervous about what a small fish like me was thinking about getting into this big pool," he recalls.

As he was walking into the party, however, he ran into yet another Deepdale member waiting at the entrance. "Mr. O'Callaghan," Chernack said, turning to the man, a legend on the floor of the New York Stock Exchange and who was now retired. The two fell in talking. Over the course of the evening, Chernack ran into a handful of Deepdale members. Among them was a member who happened to serve on the board of Allianz, the large financial services company. The member introduced Chernack to an Allianz executive named Steve Maginn. As it happens, Maginn was trying to teach his sons how to play golf. Chernack volunteered to help. Over the next three months, Maginn and Chernack talked or messaged each other almost daily about golf. Finally, Maginn asked Chernack about his career plans.

Today, Chernack is an investment specialist at Allianz. He's also the resident golf teacher. He's discovered that playing golf can not only help him get ahead in business but that he can use his passion for the game to help others succeed. He enrolled dozens of colleagues in a golf program, which he taught. Even now, on weekday evenings, he can often be found at the driving range on nearby Randall's Island or in a conference room coaching novice golfers on their swings and instructing them on the rules of the game.

Has this made him more successful as a salesman? Without a doubt, golf has become a great tool. But it is not a tool to be used as a blunt instrument. It is a tool that can help him develop bonds with people. "It isn't about taking someone out to Winged Foot or getting a client drunk," he says. "Eventually, we will do work together. But I do this in a very soft way. I take a quiet, long-term approach."

What I noticed about Chernack is that he's a generous teacher. I have no doubt that he hopes his golf acumen will translate into business. But no one wants to be pounced on by a slick-talking salesman. Chernack has learned the importance of being subtle.

The golf course is not the C-suite

My friend Steve Kelleher, the head professional at the River Course on Kiawah Island, has been lucky enough to golf with some of the most successful business people in the country. He's seen their competitive streaks on full display and he's been able to peer into their weaknesses and fears like no fellow executive ever could. So I asked Steve about the common characteristics he sees when executives are on the links. He offered these thoughts on how to improve your business golf experience:

- Don't be an "engineer." We know it's great to like to build things and analyze every step of the process. But executives who come from highly technical backgrounds often overthink the game. "Engineers can be difficult to play with. They have a tendency to expect perfection and as soon as they hit one bad shot they start to completely tear apart their swing instead of realizing that *nobody* hits every shot perfectly. But in their minds, once a swing fails to execute a shot properly then the entire swing is defective and must be rebuilt. While many perfectionists do become very accomplished players, they may not be the player of choice when you are looking for an enjoyable time on the links."

- Learn how to set expectations for golf just like you do

for your business. You will not become a single digit player by merely taking a few lessons and playing a couple times a month. "While they may have spent 8 to 12 years on advanced education and another 10 to 20 gaining practical knowledge in their respective field, they seem to think that they can shortcut the process when it comes to golf. There is a lot more to shooting low scores than just being able to hit solid golf shots just as there is more to running a business than being able to read a balance sheet."

- When it comes to customer golf, borrow a page from your sales guy. "In my experience, salesmen are the most entertaining to play golf with. They are more focused on the overall experience than they are on their own golf game. A competitive match with a salesman is usually a lot more fun, regardless of whether or not you win."

LESSON 16

Be careful whom you step on.

Below the Grass Ceiling

I WAS STANDING on a grassy hill at the posh Ritz-Carlton in Lake Las Vegas, Nevada, watching Hall of Fame golfers Jan Stephenson and Jane Blalock hit short irons to an artificial green floating in the middle of a lake. Nearby, some of the most powerful women in business were watching, practicing their swings, or talking with one another about seminars they had attended on global security and mentorship. Among those gathered for *Fortune* magazine's annual women's summit were such notables as Arianna Huffington and Iman.

Actually, I was something of a gate-crasher. My wife was an invited guest but before she left me in the hotel room she informed me that I'd have to stay out of the seminars because men were not allowed. Even for the golf clinic, I needed to keep out of sight. Then one evening, after dining by myself, I needed to pass through the entire group while they were eating dinner.

I stepped around the edges of the room but was suddenly spotted by my wife, who signaled me over. The women at her table included the very charming president of iVillage, Deborah Fine, and Donna Orender, president of the Women's National Basketball Association. Here we were in a room packed full of women who were at the top of the corporate ranks—CEOs, entrepreneurs, top investment bankers. They were talking about business and the economy and family and golf. It struck me that they seemed to bring the same qualities to the table as their male counterparts. And so I wondered, "Have the days of glass-ceiling golf ended?"

Quite a few years ago, when I was a college student and my mother was an aspiring executive at a major corporation, she called me in my dorm room to tell me that she had been promoted to vice president, making her one of the highest-ranking women in the history of the company. My mother has always been my corporate hero and my golf pal. Growing up, we'd spend summer vacations golfing in New Hampshire. I remember the time my great-grandmother was staying with us and we went to play golf. My great-grandmother sat on a terrace overlooking the first tee of our small club while we went to play. When my mother stepped up to hit, a man next to my great-grandmother sighed and said, "Oh great, a woman." To which my great-grandmother responded, "That's not any woman. That's my granddaughter you're talking about." My mother promptly swatted one of her trademark shots down the middle. She never cared much for people who told her she wasn't supposed to succeed.

My mother started as a secretary at a prominent magazine company and rose to become a top executive at another. Along the way, she endured the usual chauvinism that working women experienced in the 1960s and 1970s. She became known as a straight shooter, someone who stood her ground as an executive.

She didn't care if there was a glass ceiling because she worked hard enough the break through any barriers. When she called to tell me about the promotion, I remember crying because I knew how much it meant to her. We all want validation and this was the ultimate. One of the first occasions in this new post was a golf event the company held every year. The event included all the top customers. Her male predecessor, a novice golfer, had traditionally been invited. Since my mother was an avid golfer who talked openly about her love of the game she expected to be invited. But there was to be no such invitation. When she inquired, her counterpart at the company explained that the event was only for golfers and asked rhetorically, "You're not a golfer, are you?"

Yet I assumed, incorrectly I know now, that the golf course is no longer a barrier for women. For certain, women are more visible in golf. The Executive Women's Golf Association reports that 73 percent of female professionals who play say that golf benefits them in business. The group also reports that 22 percent have done deals on the course or at a golf club and that 67 percent believe playing golf raises their level of confidence in business. And we now see more grassroots groups with names like Chicks with Sticks and the High Tee Society. Men themselves have become avid viewers of the LPGA Tour. The notion of women's exclusion from the game seemed antiquated in 2002 when a feminist advocate named Martha Burke launched a protest against Augusta National, which called for a boycott of companies that sponsored the Masters. Burke was angry because Augusta's 300 or so members were all men and the club was generally known to have a male-only policy. Most of us in the media, with the exception of some intrepid reporters at the *New York Times*, argued that Burke had missed the point. Golf wasn't about business, we contended. It was about *relationships*. I remember telling this to Burke and explaining that I know women who have played Augusta and say they were treated with the utmost graciousness. I assumed Augusta, Pine Valley, and other male-only courses were just about guys being guys.

But then I found myself talking about this issue to several of the women at the conference—extremely successful women. And they were telling me stories just like the one my mother experienced. "I never get invited to the outings," said the CEO of one prominent company. "They invite my husband."

When I returned home, I called a friend who happens to be a senior executive of a large financial services firm. I asked her if what I was hearing made sense, and she seemed a little surprised by the question. Then she explained why. She had worked at Credit Suisse First Boston (CSFB) when the CEO was a dynamic man named John Mack. People adore Mack. He's now CEO of Morgan Stanley and is very much a gentleman and an inspirational leader. When he was running CSFB, he organized a series of events designed to introduce female executives to golf as a tool for business. These events attracted media attention and made Mack appear like an enlightened figure on Wall Street at a time when lawsuits alleging sexual discrimination were swirling around the Street. My friend, who boasts a competitive handicap and is an accomplished athlete, certainly thought Mack was on her side as she was sitting on the jet that flew her to North Carolina with other CSFB female executives. But when they arrived at the club they discovered that a cadre of male executives had already played 18 holes with the boss. Over the next day, the women took a lesson on the driving range and played the short course while the men played the *real* course. Several women found the distinction insulting. Mack probably never realized this was a snub. But it was. "They barely let us get past the driving range," my friend confided. "It was humiliating watching all the men go out and play, because many of them were awful golfers."

Those words spoken to my mother came flashing back to me. *"You don't play golf, do you?"* Those are such condescending words—expressed with such faux graciousness. The issue wasn't that these women wanted to bust up Augusta or Pine Valley and make all the male members take sewing classes and color coordinate their socks and shirts. In fact, most women I know have no problem if men want to hang out with men. Where they have a problem is when this involves business. And make no mistake, the top clubs are about business. Mack himself has made a habit of appointing golf friends to the board at Morgan Stanley, where he now works. The fact that the chairmen and CEOs of dozens of major corporations are members of Augusta National is no mere coincidence. As much as Augusta's powerful membership would like to pretend that all they are doing is playing golf, the fact is that golf is one of the least benefits of being a member. Augusta, Pine Valley, and most of the other prestigious male-only clubs are like majestic, genteel proving grounds for business deals.

Yes, women are more involved in golf than ever before. But despite the growing number of women in the ranks of senior management, the golf course is still viewed as a playground for men. And without the ability to interact in that setting—to broach the subject of a deal in that "I'm not talking business" way or to bring favored clients for a weekend in the Augusta cabins—women are at a disadvantage. And unless this attitude changes, golf will be sacrificing generations of new players.

Perhaps the key is to do what my mother did. She stood her ground. She refused to collaborate with the men who excluded her. Years later, no one leaves her out of golf events. And the fellows who decided not to extend an invitation? They're all gone.

Golf is about being humble
(and never losing hope)

Arguably, no one has more influence on the $30 trillion bond market than Bill Gross, chief investment officer of Pimco. The blackjack player turned mutual fund king has made billions for investors and sways the market with his words. As a golfer, Gross has one claim to infamy: He just about killed Tiger Woods playing at Pebble Beach with a wayward iron shot.

"My definition of being happy has always been something to do, someone to love, and something to hope for. Golf epitomizes two of those things but especially hope. Hope is a perfect reflection of golf. For 20 years, I've gone home after a day at the range and told my wife, Sue, that I've found the secret. She'll patiently ask me what that is and I'll patiently explain what I found. Then the next time I'll come home depressed and tell her that I've lost it.

"[But,] I never lose hope. There is an endless quest for the golden ring. Golfers are inherently hopeful that their game will get better, that they'll get that hole in one. It is something that will never be attained in a total way, much like Tiger will never shoot a 58, but we never stop hoping that we can do it. .

"Golf teaches me to contain my frustration. I learn that I can't always get what I want but, as the Stones said, 'If you try real hard you get what you need.' That helps me think about business, too. On any trading day when I've employed a strategy, I might be losing millions of dollars. I'll go home at night and regroup. It's like moving to the next tee. I'll go into my library and analyze what went wrong and then head into the new day."

LESSON 17

"Business" is not a bad word.

Conclusion:
Wining, Dining, and
Doing the Deal

SEVERAL YEARS AGO, an investment banker named Ken Moelis arranged for dozens of his best clients to spend time in a very special retreat at Pebble Beach. Moelis, head of investment banking at UBS and prominent as Donald Trump's banker, is one of the most powerful figures in finance and has taken countless companies public over the last 20 years. For much of this time, Pebble Beach has been a lab of sorts—a proving ground for learning more about the needs of his clients and making sure they knew him. On this occasion, Moelis went a step further. In addition to playing golf, he converted Pebble's driving range into a soccer field and flew in the U.S. Women's Soccer Team to compete against his clients. Afterward, there were drinks and a lot of laughs. "It's about fun," Moelis told me after the event. "It's not about business."

That comment made me think. Not about business? Did he

mean that UBS paid tens of thousands of dollars just to make people happy? And then I ran across an article that originally ran in *Fortune* in October 1954. This explained it all to me:

> Few businessmen like to admit, even to themselves, that mercenary motives have anything to do with their pursuit of golf. Most of them play the game because they love it. . . . That it may be good for business is so much velvet. . . . But it is simply a fact of life that golf is one of the most delightful dodges yet discovered for multiplying contacts, for ingratiating oneself with clients, and for generally enhancing one's business prestige.

A half century later, I could write the same paragraph. I can't tell you how many times I've interviewed executives who insist that they never do business on the golf course. They practically run scared from the notion that they might have some motive other than friendly competition and appreciation of a natural setting. None other than Donald Trump made that statement to me. *Donald Trump.* Who is he kidding? Trump once saved his business from financial disaster after being paired for 18 holes with a big-money lender who ended up giving him a break. Like Trump, most executives speak about the role of golf in business in sweeping generalizations. Golf, they say, teaches you about character. Whether a person plays laterally out of the woods or attempts a shot between tree limbs will tell you how they behave in the corporate suite. Someone who takes too many mulligans can't be trusted.

Those things are all true. Golf is, as I've said throughout the book, a litmus test for character and personality. But it is also a great way to get business done. Those who say otherwise are fooling only themselves. Just consider what executives say when they aren't being quoted. In *Golf Digest*'s popular semiannual report on CEO golfers, 71 percent of *Fortune* 1000 chiefs said they've ended up doing business with someone they've met on the course. Another survey, this one by Starwood Hotels, reported that 92 percent of executives believe that golf is a good way to make business contacts, 50 percent say golf is the most useful tool for getting to know clients, and 45 percent believe that playing golf with clients will yield more business.

Why else would a company like Lucent Technologies build its own golf course? In the late 1990s, Lucent spent $40 million building a country club on a 5,000-acre estate in New Jersey. The purpose was to offer memberships to Lucent's business partners at $1 million apiece plus annual fees topping several hundred thousand dollars. Though this plan backfired after the stock market collapsed and Lucent's business dried up, other companies continue to operate high-end private facilities. The insurance giant AIG operates Morefar in Brewster, New York. Located about 60 miles from Manhattan, it is one of the most private places you can ever visit. Fewer than 20 foursomes a day play the course. These consist of AIG clients and a select handful of corporate members who pay a hefty fee for limited access. Every group that goes out has been arranged for the purpose of accomplishing some sort of goal in business. "It is supposed to be business," a senior executive once told the *New York Times*. "There's no free lunch." Reports are that senior management gets to review the guest list. How is that not about business?

But what's wrong with having business as a motive? Such a comment would be considered uncouth inside the most prestigious golf clubs. Members of Cypress Point, Pine Valley, and Augusta National feel duty-bound to state that they play golf for the love of the game and it is just a coincidence that they might be paired with a client. This belies the fact that membership is practically an annuity for corporate success. How is that so? Customers who are invited to play any of these courses are much less likely to stop doing business with the member's firm because that would also mean they can't walk the fairways. One executive I know who belongs to Augusta National flies clients to the course for two days at a time. When the client arrives, he is greeted at the end of famed Magnolia Lane by a porter who already knows his name. He's then invited to lunch while his bags are brought to a special guest cottage. After lunch, the client and host go out for 18 holes followed by drinks and dinner. The next morning they play another 18 holes before leaving. The experience is unparalleled and it *is* about business. Nor is it an isolated situation. Augusta's ranks are filled with business titans who use the club as a quasicorporate membership. General Electric and American Express are just two of the companies whose CEOs become Augusta members for generations.

Business is not a four-letter word. It should not be an evil thing to use golf as a tool for business. Quite the contrary; if the goal is to understand what another person is about, there is no better tool. I've used this tool myself plenty of times. The truth is, there's no shame in admitting it. Now the last thing any of us wants is a sleazy sales guy trying to get us to sign a deal just because he took us golfing. Nor do we want to spend time with those fellows who try to impress us with how important they are. Curt Culver, the CEO of MGIC Investment Corporation and arguably the best golfer in the *Fortune* 1000, recalls that on several occasions his playing partners have had their secretaries call in with "emergency" messages. He makes a personal note not to do biz with such people. Culver himself owes his career to golf. "I can't tell you how important golf has been to my career," he says. "I've only worked at two companies—MGIC and, before that, a competitor. The chairman of the first company where I worked was an avid player. He'd seen me in some local tournaments when I was still in school. He loved to compete, so he liked to go out and play with me. I got to know him real well, and that led to a job. Golf has also helped me get to know customers and senior management. I've been out there with customers I was leery of and then once we played golf we became personal friends."

And that is the point. We spend so much time in our offices negotiating business that we often fail to really know the person on the other side of the table. If golf is an excuse to know that person better and draw some relevant conclusions about whether they can be trusted and, yes, to do more business with we shouldn't be considered uncouth in saying so.

Business happens. That's a fact. Disney agreed to acquire Capital Cities/ABC in a $19 billion deal in 1995 because of golf. Disney CEO Michael Eisner and Cap Cities's Tom Murphy ran into each other in a parking lot at the Sun Valley Resort. Murphy and companion Warren Buffett, who happened to be Cap Cities's largest shareholder, were heading out for a round of golf. The three got to chatting and the rest is history. For the most part, these deals were inadvertent. Like the discovery of penicillin, no one planned them.

Where people are mistaken is in thinking they can go out and force a situation. The Internet is packed full of articles and advice from so-called business golf experts who teach seminars to major corporations. The goal is to use golf to boost sales. I suppose that instead of measuring return on investment they must measure return on putts. No doubt, learning how to play golf with people who matter and developing pregame strategies for when to make the pitch are useful techniques for some. As is the business golf mantra that you "never talk business before the fifth hole or after the fifteenth." Though this might be helpful to know if you are playing in a corporate outing, the truth is that if you want to truly succeed in business you should not plan to pitch anything on the golf course. Let things evolve. Just like you can't *make* yourself birdie that treacherous par-4, you can't plan to consummate a transaction. If you go out with business as the focus, you will fail because your playing partners will realize that you only see them as a figure on a quarterly financial statement.

As businesspeople, we should strive to understand each other as *people*. Too often, mergers are consumated and the marrying CEOs have no idea whether they actually like each other. A round of golf would have answered that question. If you can't stand watching another player's preshot routine or you're shocked when they follow a bad shot by hurling a 5 iron into a lake, chances are you don't want to see them every day at the office.

I'd like to leave you with a final thought. Golf is one of those games where you can buy all the best equipment, join all the right private clubs, and play with all the right people—and still fall on your face. If you seek to impress or land that big deal on the green, you will fail. The game can uncover a phony faster than an errant drive can find a water hazard. The key in business and golf is to play and work with sincerity, passion, and humility. In so doing, you will find the success you seek.

LESSON 18

Never forget: it's about friendship.

Checklist on the Dos and Don'ts of Business Golf

FOLLOWING THE INITIAL PUBLICATION of this book in 2007, a number of readers asked me for practical advice on how to pursue their own deals on the green. So as parting words, let me offer the following suggestions.

- Don't go to the course expecting to do business. Your playing partner, whether a prospective client or an existing one, does not want to endure an 18-hole sales pitch. My advice is to show up planning to have a good time and let the business happen naturally. Use the experience to create a level of comfort and trust. In my own life this has worked fabulously. I've met a variety of clients and colleagues on the golf course and I've used golf to learn about people. I did this with planning but not pressure.

- Have a goal for the outcome. When playing business golf, I ask myself in advance what I hope to accomplish. Is the person I am meeting someone I want as a client? What is it that I hope to learn about them? Though I believe in planning, as mentioned above, I strongly disagree with making a pitch on the course unless your playing partner asks for one. I recommend doing a small amount of advance work aimed at eliciting certain responses. For example, if your playing partner is in real estate or manufacturing, there's a natural conversation about the economy that can segue into a greater exchange about business. Make the conversation about their views and not your opinions. This will show the person that you have an interest in what they think.

- Cater to egos. Most CEOs I've met have gigantic egos. So even though a deal isn't on the table, you should still understand some key things about your playing partner. Do a quick Google search to learn about their interests. A CEO is likely to be involved in a charity or industry trade group, for instance. Much like you would if you were planning a cocktail party, have a few topics to talk about in case the conversation runs dry. While this doesn't need to be specific to their business, most people like to talk about themselves. One caveat: Don't make the person feel like you had the FBI run a background check on them. Be subtle.

- Remember that you aren't a PGA Tour member. As my friend Steve Kelleher, who is head pro at the River Course on Kiawah Island, explained earlier in this book, he has lost count of the number of successful business people who fail to understand why they aren't successful on the course. Nothing will turn off playing partners more than a sourpuss who complains about every shot.

- Know whether your playing partners are serious or funny. While I like to laugh a lot on the course, I've also learned—the hard way—that not everyone is as relaxed on the course. I was playing with an investment banker not long ago. He was fairly intense from the start, making it obvious that he didn't heed my advice above. At 18, he topped his ball in the water. I commented that he "hit that one with the ugly stick"—something friends and I say all the time. Rather than laugh, the fellow proceeded to slam his iron repeatedly into the turf. He walked off the 18th green and refused to shake my hand. He might have been a jerk, but it was still a lost opportunity if I'd wanted to do business with him.

- Guys, don't be sexist. (And ladies, don't be afraid that you aren't good enough.) As I mentioned earlier, many male bosses still have a hard time realizing that professional women are often avid golfers—and are sometimes much better than men. Sexism is obviously not a good thing. Aside from a practical matter it will eliminate the opportunity to meet prospective business partners based on gender alone.

- Public courses can be just as good as private ones. Don't get hung up on the idea that you have to belong to a country club. In many places, public courses now exceed private ones in terms of quality of the facilities. I'm not even talking about Pebble Beach. My father and I have played a public course in Middlefield, Connecticut, that charges less than $50 a round. One time the starter paired us with another twosome that included the CEO of a major casino company. We had a great round and I learned about his opinions of various competitors.

- Save the alcoholic beverages for the 19th hole. A friend told me about a time when he went out with two colleagues who proceeded to drink two six-packs each. The inebriated duo probably thought they were just having a great time. My friend, however, felt uncomfortable with the heavy drinking and left the course with a negative impression of his colleagues.

- Remember that there is no magic formula for doing business on the golf course. Every person will give you a special opportunity. So be flexible and open to nuances.

Beyond these suggestions, the most important advice I can give anyone is that you be true to yourself. I've seen a lot of players, particularly salespeople, who morph into something they are not when they get onto the golf course. That is a sure way to set yourself up for failure if your playing partner ever wants to do business with you.

Acknowledgments

In the fall of 2005, I received a call from Adrienne Schultz that made this book a reality. Adrienne, who is an editor at Portfolio, told me she'd read the outline for a book I wanted to write about golf and business. The outline had been making the rounds at her company when it landed on her desk. It was a pretty messy draft of a few chapters and ideas. But Adrienne and her boss, Adrian Zackheim, were supportive throughout the entire process and have earned my gratitude and respect.

There are many others who advised me and endured my occasional moments of panic and frequent desire to stop writing and go play golf. One of the best people I've met in recent years is my agent, Esmond Harmsworth. Esmond is part mentor, part drill sergeant but always has a gentleman's touch. Others who were instrumental in this book were Karen Bacot, Steve Kelleher, and J. J. Butcher at Kiawah Island; John Steinbach at TaylorMade-adidas;

and Ron Mortirano, my first advocate at Penguin. Don Durgin, who, sadly, passed away in 2003, was a great friend who guided me through the intricacies of private golf clubs. My friend Bill Norton provided excellent background. My brother-in-law Gary Vickers, the funniest man in Greene County, Georgia, made sure to keep me fully stocked with off-color stories from his own days on the fairways.

I owe a special note of gratitude to John Atwood, editor in chief at *T&L Golf,* who first hired me to write a column about business and allowed me to use those contributions in this book. John is a true ambassador of the game. Hank Gilman, the deputy managing editor at *Fortune,* and general counsel Laury Frieber also allowed me to adapt several articles I'd written for the magazine. Hank and former *Fortune* senior editor Erik Torkells, who now runs *Budget Travel,* were instrumental in enabling me to use my perch as a writer and my love of golf to venture out into the business community and learn things about people I never could have seen from the opposite side of a conference table.

My family also played a major role. I'd like to thank my parents, Mary Sue and Nick, for putting up with a nagging kid who just had to play golf and for never mentioning out loud that practicing on the range after sunset is a little extreme. My father and mother taught me that the game is about family and fun. My grandfather "Big Julie" Harburger taught me that you're never too old to knock a 3 wood onto a green. And my great-grandmother taught me that what matters is where the ball comes to a rest—not how ugly the trip was getting there.

Finally, to the greatest foursome. I wouldn't be anything in writing, business, or life without my wife, Marcia Vickers, and our two sons, Christopher and Carter. It's when I'm out on the course with these two fine young men that I'm reminded of my own lesson: Golf is about being with friends.

Index